The 3ʳᵈ Reformation of the Church

Are you ready for it?

The revolution has begun!

Church...like you've been waiting your whole life for!

DR BRAD NORMAN

Now Word Publishing, Salvation House, Unit 2 Sterling Court, Mundells, Welwyn Garden City, Hertfordshire, AL7 1FT

www.nowwordpublishing.co.uk

ISBN: 978-0-9929519-0-0

Cover Design: SFTN Media
Editing: Hayley Bandy

Printed in the United Kingdom

Contents: Page:

Prologue   5

DEDICATION:

I wish to dedicate this book to the two people who have most helped in shaping and moulding my life and ministry; Dr Fred and Pastor Nellie Roberts. As I seek to follow the mandate and path of destiny the Lord has set before me, I continue to daily benefit from the life skills I developed and godly counsel I gain from these amazing spiritual parents. Not just your words but your lives are an example to me of true apostleship and servanthood. The life of faith you have led inspires me to believe - that with God nothing is impossible! To Wyona and me...you are living legends!

APPRECIATION:

I wish to thank the incredible people who are Salvation for the Nations International Churches for your commitment to pursue God's call to reformation with me. Thank you for your trust...thank you for your willingness to change and embrace new ways of thinking about and doing church! God has called us to do this - together! Thank you to my wife, Wyona and children, all of whom share in ministry with me. You are my A TEAM!

PROLOGUE:

It has been my privilege over the past twenty-five years to have served the Body of Christ in full-time pastoral ministry. I have served in diverse settings, namely; full-time military chaplaincy, as pastor of mainline denominational as well as independent charismatic churches. These years have been an adventure and a journey of discovery.

Many today, like me, are frustrated and find themselves questioning how authentic Christians really are. Many even feel guilty over their waning enthusiasm about church attendance and participation. There are also those who feel dissatisfied with their own spiritual growth and progress. Many members struggle with the issue of how relevant their faith is in their everyday lives and how the Kingdom of God, His influence and rule, is expressed and demonstrated, in their homes, their work place or even their church.

We claim to believe in an omnipresent, omniscient and omnipotent God Who has sent His Holy Spirit, not just to be with us, but in us (John 14:16-17) and poured out His power upon His Church (Acts 2:1-21). However, the experience of many today is: "Hi, welcome to church. Here's your bulletin. We'll get you out in an hour. See you next week." Surely, Jesus had something more in mind when He said,

"I will build My church" (Matt. 16:18)? How different would today's church be, if we stopped trying to control it and let the Holy Spirit have His way? I believe this is exactly what the world needs to experience!

So here's the reason I wrote this book...not as a critique on all that's wrong with today's Church, but because:

- I believe the "harvest is ripe", that this is an hour of great opportunity and every local church has the potential to reach this generation and change the world. "Do you not say, 'There are still four months and *then* comes the harvest'? Behold, I say to you, lift up your eyes and look at the fields, for they are already white for harvest" (John 4:35).
- I believe that the methods may change, but the message never changes. "The grass withers, the flower fades, but the word of our God stands forever" (Isa. 40:8). The only way to facilitate real change in society and impact nations is through the Unchanging Gospel, "But even if we, or an angel from heaven, preach any other gospel to you than what we have preached to you, let him be accursed" (Gal. 1:8).
- I believe that some of the greatest leaders that the world will ever know are currently in our primary and secondary schools; making ministry to youth and children one of the greatest mission opportunities that the local church can invest in. "Train up a child in the way he should go, and when he is old he will not depart from it" (Prov. 22:6).

- I believe that more and more church leaders are going to lay aside prejudices and personal preferences of ministry and work together with others in Kingdom and Apostolic relationships to accomplish more than they could have ever done alone. (Deut. 32:29-30) "Oh, that they were wise, *that* they understood this, *that* they would consider their latter end! [30] How could one chase a thousand, And two put ten thousand to flight, unless their Rock had sold them, and the Lord had surrendered them?"

- I believe that we're going to experience one of the greatest moves of God this generation has ever witnessed, in the next decade, because the local church finally decided to step up and be the Church it was destined and created to be; before the foundation of the world. "Blessed *be* the God and Father of our Lord Jesus Christ, who has blessed us with every spiritual blessing in the heavenly *places* in Christ, [4] just as He chose us in Him before the foundation of the world, that we should be holy and without blame before Him in love" (Eph. 1:3-4).

- I believe God has called the Church to CHANGE the world...not complain about it! We are His anointed and empowered people, whom He has called to attempt the "impossible" so that people can see Him. "But Jesus looked at *them* and said to them, "With men this is impossible, but with God all things are possible" (Matt. 19:26). So...what is it that you know you should do next? Read on...

CHAPTER 1:   WHAT IS THE 3RD REFORMATION?

God is constantly restoring His Church. That restoration will continue right up to the moment Christ returns! In that restoration of the Church there have been at least two great reformations. Each reformation has had several restorational moves within it.

God's purpose in the First Reformation was to birth and establish His Church, activate and empower it to touch the entire world. That took place through the coming of Jesus; through His revolutionary teaching and miracles, through the shedding of His blood on the cross, through sending the Holy Spirit at Pentecost and through the ministry of the first apostles and the Early Church.

The purpose of the Second Reformation, which started with the Protestant Movement and Martin Luther, was to activate and to liberate the Church out of the Dark Ages. Following this, God raised up many denominations and church movements to continue to move the Church forward in His purpose and plan.

I believe that the Church is now experiencing a Third Reformation and in this present reformation, God is releasing new power, authority and grace. There have been many restorations of truth bringing us into this reformation such as: The Apostolic and

Prophetic Movement, the Saints Movement, the restoration of the Message of Grace, the understanding of Market-Place Ministry and so on...

In essence, it is (Rev. 11:15) "The kingdoms of this world have become (the Greek is 'ginomai' ...'are becoming' ...it's a movement towards) the kingdoms of this world (are becoming) the kingdoms of our Lord and of His Christ, and He shall reign forever and ever!" This reformation is bringing about a paradigm shift in the goal and purpose of the Church.

The fact is that most Evangelicals, Charismatics and Pentecostals see no mandate for the Church beyond evangelising the "unsaved". That will never change! That will always be the primary purpose, the Great Commission, (Matt. 28:19) to "Go therefore and make disciples of all the nations, baptizing them in the name of the Father and of the Son and of the Holy Spirit".

However, in addition to that, the Third Reformation Church is returning to its responsibility to co-labour with Christ to manifest His Kingdom! God is bringing the Church back to the understanding and practice that:

- All believers are priests; they all have spiritual gifts and a purpose. Every believer is called to do the work of the ministry. Spiritual Gifts and the Gifts of the Spirit are for today and every believer is to operate in the Spiritual Gifts and Gifts of the Spirit given to them. All believers can flow and function in signs, wonders, miracles and the power of God.

- All believers are called not just to be priests but to be kings of the Kingdom of God, for (Rev. 1:6) says, "And has made us kings and priests...to His God and Father". That we are called not just to wait for the Rapture to come, but to exercise His Kingdom influence, to change and bring social transformation to our cities, nations and our world.

(Rev. 5:10) says, "And have made us kings and priests to our God; and we shall (do what? ...we shall) reign on the earth." The Church has largely believed and taught that that will only happen after the Second Coming or after the Rapture, or after the Tribulation, or after the Millennial Reign of Christ. It is important to emphasize here, that by this, I do not mean, as some Dominionists wrongfully apply this; that man is commissioned to bring the entire world under the dominion of Christianity, by force if necessary, and then, hand over the Christianized world to Jesus when He comes. Some elements of Dominionism even falsely claim that Jesus CANNOT return until all His enemies have been put under the feet of the Church.

A major part of this reformation is the correct understanding that the Kingdom of God, which is the "Reign of God", began when Jesus was raised from the dead and ascended to the Right Hand of the Father. That the Kingdom is coming through continual outpourings of the Holy Spirit and through the works of the saints/believers, because Jesus said in (John 14:12] "Most assuredly, I say to you, he who believes in Me, the works that I do he will do also; and greater works than these he will do, because I go to my Father" and that the fullness of the Kingdom will come at Jesus' final return!

However, Jesus taught us to pray in the Lord's Prayer (Matt. 6:9-13) for God's Kingdom to come, now! "Your kingdom come. Your will be done on earth as *it is* in heaven" (verse 10). Therefore, in this reformation God is raising up the kings of the Kingdom and releasing the priests of the Kingdom. That their ministry is not just on a Sunday within the four walls of a church building, or in the mid-week meeting or home group, but that they have been empowered, called and commissioned to be the Church, 24/7, manifesting the Kingdom of God wherever they live and work!

Releasing and charging them to reclaim and retake the 7 Mountains or 7 key areas of influence in the world. Theocracy is not to be confused with theocratic government but rather the goal to have "Kingdom-minded people" in all areas of society. We have to be a godly voice to stop the decay; we have to illuminate the path of truth and the way to salvation. There are seven areas identified specifically: (1.) the **Business Mountain,** (2.) the **Mountain of Government,** (3.) the **Family Mountain,** (4.) the **Church/Religious Mountain,** (5.) the **Media Mountain,** (6.) the **Education Mountain** and (7.) the **Mountain of Arts and Entertainment.**

We have to invade, retake and reclaim these territories, because it is there that our culture, that our generation will be won or lost! This Third Reformation is about getting the Church back into every one of those areas of influence; to reach people with the message of the Gospel! These will be dealt with in greater detail in chapter 7.

There is a great flow of apostolic restoration taking place all over the world today with apostolic ministries being established throughout the nations. One of the most significant restorational movements leading up to this Third Reformation has been the New Apostolic Reformation. Those who call the New Apostolic Reformation a cult reveal their ignorance of Scripture and limited understanding of Ecclesiology. The NAR embraces the Apostles' Creed and all the standard classic statements of Christian doctrine. In fact the NAR encompasses the largest non-Catholic component of world Christianity. It is in addition, the most rapidly growing component of the Church and the only component of Christianity that presently is increasing at a faster rate than the world population.

Christianity is flourishing now in the Global South which includes sub-Saharan Africa, Latin America, and large parts of Asia. Most of the new churches in the Global South, even including many which belong to denominations, would comfortably fit into the New Apostolic Reformation ethos and model.

The primary distinctive of the NAR is that it represents the most radical change in the way of doing church since the Protestant Reformation. It must be stressed that these are not doctrinal changes. The NAR adheres to the major tenets of the Reformation, such as; the authority of Scripture, justification by faith, and the priesthood of all believers. But the practical expression of the Christian life both within the local church and society, the way the church is governed, the expressions of worship, the theology of prayer, the missional goals, the optimistic vision for the future, and other characteristics, are significantly different from traditional Protestantism.

This reformation, I believe, will move and develop this apostolic restoration still further. We are entering the Third Great Reformation of the Church and it will not be just about the emergence of new and dynamic Five-fold ministries, but rather, I believe we will see Apostolic Teams arising and for the first time, since the days of Acts, a fully functional Five-fold Ministry operating together and no longer as separate entities.

WHAT THE THIRD REFORMATION IS NOT:
I believe it is of absolute importance to clarify what the Third Reformation is not, before there is the temptation to dismiss and wrongfully align a crucial restoration of truth, with other movements, which, although they contain elements of truth, have moved beyond the boundaries of acceptable biblical interpretation and application.

Many of these movements began at the point of restoration of truth but on some key element wrongfully diverted from the revelation of Scripture. The unfortunate consequence to this was that it was out-rightly rejected by the wider church, and as the saying goes, "the baby was thrown out with the bathwater". In other words, those elements of truth that were needed to be heard and rightfully applied were also rejected.

It is also important to recognise that many of these misapplications of restored truth occurred not at a primary but at a secondary level and beyond. By that I mean that those individuals, who rightfully discerned the truth for that time, cannot in every instance, be held accountable for those who would take that teaching to the extreme, or manipulate it for their own purposes and agendas. In many instances, this has unfortunately been the case.

THE THIRD REFORMATION DOES NOT ASSERT:

- That Christian should work NOW toward either a world/nation governed by Christians or one governed by a conservative Christian understanding of biblical law – also known as Christian Reconstructionism. Jesus clearly said in (John 18:36), "My kingdom is not of this world. If My kingdom were of this world, My servants would fight, so that I should not be delivered to the Jews; but now My kingdom is not from here".

- That the Church must gain control of the earth's governmental and social institutions, and establish the Kingdom on earth; then, and only then, can Jesus come - also known as Theocratic Government. When He returns the government will be on His shoulders not ours. "For unto us a Child is born, unto us a Son is given; and the government will be upon His shoulder. And His name will be called Wonderful, Counselor, Mighty God, Everlasting Father, Prince of Peace.[7] Of the increase of *His* government and peace *there will be* no end, upon the throne of David and over His kingdom, to order it and establish it with judgment and justice from that time forward, even forever. The zeal of the Lord of hosts will perform this" (Isa. 9:6-7).

- That the emphasis on preparation for the Rapture (1 Thess. 4:16-17) and Second Coming of Christ (Matt. 25:31-46; Rev. 19) should be replaced with a humanistic endeavour to establish a man-made millennial utopia on earth (1 Thess. 3:11-13). Paul warned the Church, in (2 Thess. 2:1-3), "Now, brethren, concerning the coming of our Lord Jesus Christ and our gathering together to Him, we ask you, [2] not to be soon shaken in mind or troubled, either by spirit or by word or by letter, as if from us, as though the day of Christ had come. [3] Let no one deceive you by any means; for *that Day will not come* unless the falling away comes first, and the man of sin is revealed, the son of perdition, [4] who opposes and exalts himself above all that is called God or that is worshiped, so that he sits as God in the temple of God, showing himself that he is God. [5] Do you not remember that when I was still with you I told you these things?"

- That the Church has replaced Israel in God's plan - also known as Replacement Theology. God has established an "everlasting covenant" with Israel that cannot be broken, "And I will establish My covenant between Me and you and your descendants after you in their generations, for an everlasting covenant, to be God to you and your descendants after you. [8] Also I give to you and your descendants after you the land in which you are a stranger, all the land of Canaan, as an everlasting possession; and I will be their God" (Gen. 17:7-8).

Though it is true that the blessings of Abraham belong now also to us (Gal. 3:29), and that the Church does replace Israel in some areas such as properly representing God on earth, acknowledging the promise of the Messiah, etc., it is not biblical to say that God is completely done with Israel and that the Christian Church is its complete replacement. "For I do not desire, brethren, that you should be ignorant of this mystery, lest you should be wise in your own opinion, that blindness in part has happened to Israel until the fullness of the Gentiles has come in. [26] And so all Israel will be saved, as it is written: "The Deliverer will come out of Zion, and He will turn away ungodliness from Jacob" (Rom. 11:25-26).

- That one-on-one evangelism (Matt. 4:19; Mark 16:15; Acts 1:8) be replaced with "Kingdom building," corporate activities for cities, regions and nations - also known as Transformational Christianity. When we minimize evangelism, neglect it, or replace it with some other "religious" activity, as men have often done, we are surely NOT following a biblical pattern. "But sanctify the Lord God in your hearts, and always *be* ready to *give* a defense to everyone who asks you a reason for the hope that is in you, with meekness and fear" (1 Pet. 3:15).

- That all "last days" Bible prophecy has already been fulfilled - also known as Preterism. "After these things I looked, and behold, a door *standing* open in heaven. And the first voice which I heard *was* like a trumpet speaking with me, saying, "Come up here, and I will show you things which MUST TAKE PLACE AFTER THIS" (Rev. 4:1).

In (Luke 19:13) Jesus told the Church to, "Occupy till I come". My question is, is the Church really occupying or are we just doing business as usual? There are great revivals in the world with hundreds of thousands being converted, but are we really occupying? I realize this is not a simple problem but one that will take the concentrated efforts of Christians across the board. How can we as Believers step across our own man-made lines and limitations and start acting as the Body of Christ as a whole and not just a lot of parts? The barriers have to come down, how can we occupy if we can't even come to agreement within ourselves. Jesus said, "And if a house is divided against itself, that house cannot stand" (Mark 3:25).

To occupy means to "drive out previous tenants and possess in their place", to "disinherit in order to inherit", to "dispossess in order to possess". To occupy is to fully influence every aspect of society as we know it, spiritually, as well as socially and economically. This kind of change doesn't just effect a generation but effects future generations as well. If you change a culture you change the very fabric of the society that people live in.

CHAPTER 2: REFORMATION3 CHURCH – CHURCH…LIKE YOU'VE BEEN WAITING YOUR WHOLE LIFE FOR!

It has been said, that if you want to write a best seller, then write a book about how the Church is messed up. It will sell well outside of the Church but it will sell even better inside the Church. You could comment on how the Church is out of date culturally, how it is too critical or too politically correct. You could discuss how it needs to contextualize its theology, or where it meets or adjust its worship style. Whoever you ask, everyone has an opinion, everyone agrees, that something has to change.

The majority of church attendees are older than the general population and men are under-represented. As evolution, humanism and atheism continue to infiltrate our schools and the media; our young people are faced with hard questions. According to some statistics, 80% to 85% of young people leave the Church, never to return. If we send our children out into the world unequipped to answer these questions and seeing their dreams for a better world and their quest to make a difference, separate and disconnected from the Church, we should not be surprised if they fall away. It's not just the young but also the older generation that are facing issues today, which the old sermonizing of the past just does not address any more. People want their faith to be relevant. People want church to be contextual and part of the solution or "why bother with it?" Statistics show, that it has now reached a critical, tipping point!

The vast majority of church leaders are not oblivious to the fact that there is something missing from the mainstream church today. The challenge is that they are unsure as to what it is! How then do you adequately address it in a meaningful and constructive way? They do not want a real "shaking". There is too much to lose. My challenge is; there is too much to gain, to miss it! That is the purpose of this book, to be a prophetic cry to the present-day church, to wake up and not miss this day of visitation! I don't write as someone who thrives on criticizing everyone else so as to establish my own spiritual superiority, or as someone who is feeding on sour grapes because things aren't the way I would like them.

I have written it because of how many people I meet on a daily basis that are discouraged by traditional church and have chosen not to attend anymore. This is not because they have turned their back on their faith, but because they are uninspired by what they see and experience. I have written it because of the increasing number of pastors I meet, some of whom have given the greater portion of their lives and spent decades in ministry, serving the church, and yet who now find themselves at a crisis point, questioning the real purpose of it all.

We are supposed to be the "salt of the earth" (Matt. 5:13), as something that preserves and gives flavour to make a meal taste good. But when we are not attracting the lost, but rather repelling them, then our salt has lost its savour. "You are the salt of the earth; but if the salt loses its flavor, how shall it be seasoned? It is then good for nothing but to be thrown out and trampled underfoot by men." What is even more troubling, is the fact that statistically, we are even repelling the saved.

We are supposed to be the "light of the world" (Matt. 5:14-16). "You are the light of the world. A city that is set on a hill cannot be hidden. [15] Nor do they light a lamp and put it under a basket, but on a lampstand, and it gives light to all *who are* in the house.[16] Let your light so shine before men, that they may see your good works and glorify your Father in heaven", and yet, on one hand we find churches that have lost their prophetic voice and become so compromising, that they excuse any sin or misconduct. On the other hand, there are those who proclaim their self-righteous judgments on everything and even every church around them, because self-preservation has become their only quest!

But in the middle, where we aspire to discover something that is more balanced, we find a church that has become socially based, smooth and sophisticated, and presented like a Broadway production so that it will appeal to the masses. What happened to the true message of repentance that brought people, by the hundreds, down to the altar to make right with God? "For I am not ashamed of the gospel of Christ, for it is the power of God to salvation for everyone who believes, for the Jew first and also for the Greek" (Rom. 1:16).

This is Christianity 101; it is the essence of the cross; it is the Great Commission that Jesus commanded us with. (Luke 24:46-48) "Then He said to them, "Thus it is written, and thus it was necessary for the Christ to suffer and to rise from the dead the third day, [47] and that repentance and remission of sins should be preached in His name to all nations, beginning at Jerusalem. [48] And you are witnesses of these things." Tragically, today, the Great Commission in many churches has become the Great Omission!

Where have all the signs, wonders and miracles gone (Acts 2:43; 5:12)? Not the watered-down "if it is God's will" (Matt. 8:2; Mark 9:22-23) or a reliance on a "gradual healing", but the instant manifestation of the power of God? "And these signs will follow those who believe: In My name they will cast out demons; they will speak with new tongues; [18] they will take up serpents; and if they drink anything deadly, it will by no means hurt them; they will lay hands on the sick, and they will recover" (Mark 16:17-18).

Jesus said to heal the sick, and preach the Gospel. Did He really mean it? Of course He meant it! Where is the outpouring of the Holy Ghost? Do we even know what it means anymore to feel the presence of the Spirit of God descend on a service and touch people in power? It's been so long since many churches have experienced the real thing that they don't even know what it is anymore. Something is wrong!

That is why God is bringing about another Great Reformation. There is a 'New Wineskin' coming. In fact it is already here. There is a new "breed" of leadership arising - many of them trained in the 'wilderness'…outside of the church…for such a time as this. Let the new leaders arise and let the existing leaders be re-awakened spiritually, re-informed in their thinking and re-formed in their mandate.

This is a "kairos moment" for the Church. History records these moments for us…so let's be part of making history and not be left behind by it. Let's be sure we do our part, led and empowered by The One who is the Head of His Church (Col. 1:18), building His Church (Matt. 16:18), perfecting it and returning for it! "That He might present her to Himself a glorious church, not having spot or wrinkle or any such thing, but that she should be holy and without blemish" (Eph. 5:27).

WHAT A 3RD REFORMATION CHURCH LOOKS LIKE:

Please note that the following is **NOT** a statement of **DOCTRINE** but is a statement of **PRACTICE**:

- A **REFORMATION3 CHURCH** acknowledges the headship of Christ and His Word as its supreme authority (Matt. 16:18; Eph. 1:22; 2:20; 5:23; Col. 1:18; Isa. 40:8; 2 Tim. 3:16; 1 Pet. 1:25).

- A **REFORMATION3 CHURCH** acknowledges that the primary purpose of the Church today is to continue Jesus' ministry as His Body on the earth (Mark 16:15-20; John 14:12; 1 Cor. 12:27-31).

- A **REFORMATION3 CHURCH** acknowledges that for Jesus' ministry to be manifest in and through the Church the full Five-fold Ministry must be acknowledged and operating (Eph. 4:11-16).

- A **REFORMATION3 CHURCH** acknowledges that every believer is called to be a priest of the Kingdom to operate in their giftings and ministries firstly to God and then to reach the lost and make disciples of all nations (Rev. 1:6; Mark 12:30-31; 1 Pet. 2:5; Rom. 12:3-8; 1 Cor. 12:1-26; Matt. 28:19-20).

- A **REFORMATION3 CHURCH** acknowledges that every believer is called to be a king of the Kingdom to operate in their giftings and ministries to exercise Jesus' dominion to change and bring social transformation to our cities, nation and our world (Gen. 1:26-28; Rev. 5:10; Matt. 5:13-16; Eph. 5:8; Matt. 16:19; 18:18).

WHAT THAT LOOKS LIKE PRACTICALLY:

It is obvious, when we look at today's Church; that the way things are is not the way Jesus initially intended them to be. He birthed His Church in the power of the Holy Spirit, and to assume, as some do, that that supernatural power and anointing was limited to that time alone is to limit God Himself. He is the God Who does not change (Mal. 3:6; Heb. 13:8).He promises us that the end of a thing will be greater than the beginning (Hag. 2:9; Acts 2:17-20). It's time we allow God to get the Church back to the position of influence it is supposed to have...to reach the lost and transform the found...to be a revolutionary movement, to change the world!

(Acts 2:42-47) "And they continued steadfastly in the apostles' doctrine and fellowship, in the breaking of bread, and in prayers. [43] Then fear came upon every soul, and many wonders and signs were done through the apostles. [44] Now all who believed were together, and had all things in common, [45] and sold their possessions and goods, and divided them among all, as anyone had need. [46] So continuing daily with one accord in the temple, and breaking bread from house to house, they ate their food with gladness and simplicity of heart, [47] praising God and having favor with all the people. And the Lord added to the church daily those who were being saved."

This is a description of the First Reformation Church and it is this dynamic operation that the Holy Spirit is re-forming in the Third Reformation Church. Without these powerful priorities the Church can never prosper, grow and impact the nations.

They are:

• **Revolutionary Devotion** - (Acts 2:42) tells us that the Church was continually devoting themselves. This tells us that the Jerusalem church was a focused church. It was a church that knew what it was supposed to be doing - and it was resolved to do it. Luke says, "they continued steadfastly"; it carries with it the idea of "devotion," "commitment," and "full dedication." Luke makes it sound as if there was nothing else that was important to these men and women. However, we are talking about people who had families to raise, jobs to attend to, everyday concerns just like you and me and yet, God tells us that they were devoted to the apostles' teaching and to fellowship, to the breaking of bread and to prayer.

In other words they were passionate about the things of God. When passion is lost, the result is that ministry becomes mechanical, worship becomes dead liturgy and Bible teaching becomes dead orthodoxy. The First Church was hungry for God's Word. The Third Reformation Church has to rediscover this passion and commitment by no longer dividing the secular with the spiritual, thereby causing people to split their loyalties. We have mistakenly measured "spirituality" by the number of hours people "clock up" at church each week, and in so doing have robbed them of their destinies! They are not just supposed to be ministering "in the church"! Rather the Third Reformation Church encourages people to connect every area of their lives; their work and their worship together, and to do all things to the glory of God (1 Cor. 10:31; Col. 3:17; 23-24).

They were devoted to God, to one another and to prayer. The early Christians believed in the power of prayer. They understood that prayer was a critical part of the health of the church in Jerusalem which is why they gathered each day to seek the will and direction of God. If any church wants to make history and change lives; prayer must become a priority again. The Third Reformation Church recognises the need for action and participation in society to bring about change, but is also convinced that nothing can succeed without prayer and makes prayer the starting place for all things! "Assuredly, I say to you, whatever you bind on earth will be bound in heaven, and whatever you loose on earth will be loosed in heaven.[19] "Again I say to you that if two of you agree on earth concerning anything that they ask, it will be done for them by My Father in heaven" (Matt. 18:18-19).

- **Revolutionary Unity** - (Acts 2:44; 46a) Real unity is when one rejoices, we all rejoice and when one hurts, we all hurt. True unity is that we don't want to compete to see who has the best this or best that, but we are only concerned and focused on the Kingdom of God and its growth. Real unity doesn't look at the social or economic status. Real unity doesn't look at race, ethnicity or gender. Real unity only sees Christ and His Kingdom and is motivated out of a desire to do my part to help the Kingdom advance. They were known for their revolutionary love which was so counter to the culture of the day, that Jesus said, "By this all will know that you are My disciples, if you have love for one another" (John 13:35).

When we return to the real reason for why we are here, why the Church exists in the first place; the issues that separate and divide pale into insignificance and we can celebrate the fact that unity is neither uniformity nor conformity, but that there is unity in diversity. We can celebrate each other's God-given uniqueness (1 Cor. 12:15-26). This was the prayer of Jesus for His Church, "I do not pray for these alone, but also for those who will believe in Me through their word; [21] that they all may be one, as You, Father, are in Me, and I in You; that they also may be one in Us, that the world may believe that You sent Me" (John 17:21). This unity so reflects the nature of God that He says that where it exists, that's where He commands the blessing (Ps. 133:1-3).

- **Revolutionary Praise and Worship** - (Acts 2:47a) Real praise arises out of a heart that is awestruck with God, "Let all the earth fear the Lord; let all the inhabitants of the world stand in awe of Him" (Ps. 33:8). When you get a revelation of Who He is, you can't help but praise Him. A lot of praise and worship in the Church today has become about the method and style more than about the purpose. God isn't impressed with the content; God is looking at the intent. Jesus said in (Matt. 15:8), "'These people draw near to Me with their mouth, and honor Me with *their* lips, but their heart is far from Me".

In some churches today, the praise and worship is more like a television talent show. Please don't misunderstand; I believe we should strive for excellence unto the Lord, (Heb. 11:14; 1 Pet. 2:12 see chpt. 9) and I believe the Church should have the best music and multi-media (Ps. 33:3). However, when, in certain "seeker sensitive" contexts, the congregation becomes an audience, watching others worship for them...something is radically wrong!

When there is so little manifestation of the "real thing" - the manifest glory of God, churches have to either resort to hype and entertainment or the other extreme; rigid, religious liturgy! God wants to powerfully encounter His people in worship again! In Acts chapter 16, Paul and Silas were definitely in need of God's presence to show up and deliver them from their unjust imprisonment. (Acts 16:25-26) says, "But at midnight Paul and Silas were praying and singing hymns to God, and the prisoners were listening to them. [26] Suddenly there was a great earthquake, so that the foundations of the prison were shaken; and immediately all the doors were opened and everyone's chains were loosed". Not only were their bonds loosed but the bonds of everyone around them were also broken.

God is looking for heartfelt praise. David said in (Ps. 9:1), "I will praise *You*, O Lord, with my whole heart". God promises to inhabit the praise of His people (Ps. 22:3). To inhabit means He wants to dwell and not just visit. God does not need our praise or our worship...He is God no matter what we do or don't do, but we do need His presence. Someone once said that praise is like "bragging" on God, because when we praise Him; we are telling Him all the great and awesome things about Himself. Praise is bragging on God's nature, attributes, character and works. Praise is agreeing with God concerning what He has already told us about Himself, what He has done, is doing and what we believe, by faith and according to His Word, He is going to do!

¹ O Lord, our Lord,
How excellent *is* Your name in all the earth,
Who have set Your glory above the heavens!
² Out of the mouth of babes and nursing infants
You have ordained strength,
Because of Your enemies,
That You may silence the enemy and the avenger.

³ When I consider Your heavens, the work of Your fingers,
The moon and the stars, which You have ordained,
⁴ What is man that You are mindful of him,

And the son of man that You visit him?
⁵ For You have made him a little lower than the angels,
And You have crowned him with glory and honor.

⁶ You have made him to have dominion over the works of Your hands;
You have put all *things* under his feet,
⁷ All sheep and oxen-
Even the beasts of the field,
⁸ The birds of the air,
And the fish of the sea
That pass through the paths of the seas.

⁹ O LORD, our Lord,
How excellent *is* Your name in all the earth! (Ps. 8)

(Heb. 13:15) says, "Therefore by Him let us continually offer the sacrifice of praise to God, that is, the fruit of *our* lips, giving thanks to His name". Praise is a sacrificial offering to God, the spiritual "first-fruits" of our lips. God is looking for people to fill His house, again, with an attitude of praise and a sincere heart of worship, so He can feel welcome to dwell in that place and manifest His power once more. He is looking for worshippers who will worship Him, "in spirit and truth" (John 4:24). The Third Reformation Church will see a significant shift back to God-centred, God-focussed worship; that touches heaven and changes earth!

• **Revolutionary Growth** - (Acts 2:47) The intent of the Gospel and the purpose of the Holy Spirit is not solely for the benefit of the Body, so that we can be built up. The purpose is for the advancement and growth of the Kingdom of God. Transfers from one church to another does not equal growth. People wanted what the disciples had. They could see the freedom that comes with being in Christ. They could plainly see the power of God at work in their lives. They were, "convicted" and responded to the preaching and were saved.

What was the result? "And that day about three thousand souls were added *to them*" (Acts 2:41). The result was that it impacted the city. They found favour with all the people of Jerusalem. At this point there was no opposition and no persecution. There was no high pressure methods used to persuade people to come and join and the people of the city saw the joy of the new followers of Christ. They saw the miracles. They saw the results of radical new lives and, longing for the same, they opened their hearts to Jesus Christ. I want you to know that when people see the power of God at work in our churches, how we love each other, operate in the spiritual gifts, our joy, our enthusiasm, it is almost irresistible! The Church will grow…it's inevitable!

I'm not saying we should throw out all of our research, strategic planning, strategies and structure. We just need to be reminded of the fact that in Jesus' Parable of the True Vine, He reminds us that without Him we cannot bear "much fruit", in fact He says we "can do nothing" (John 15:5)! If we are going to be effective we need Him to add His 'super' to our 'natural'. That is what happened in the Book of Acts, that is what happened in great moves of God throughout history, and that is what we need today. Paul said, "And my speech and my preaching *were* not with persuasive words of human wisdom, but in demonstration of the Spirit and of power, [5] that your faith should not be in the wisdom of men but in the power of God" (1 Cor. 2:4-5).

• **Revolutionary Manifestations** - (Acts 2:43) Signs, wonders and miracles are a part of the Kingdom today just as much as they were in Bible times. The reason why we don't see miracles like we used to is that in our society and in our churches, God and His power is just one of many options. In this Third Reformation we need to get to the place where God is a necessity. (Ps. 103:2-3) "Bless the Lord, O my soul, and forget not all His benefits: [3] Who forgives all your iniquities, Who heals all your diseases". If sin and sickness were a part of God's will and ultimate plan, He would never have sent His Son to die on a cross, (Isa. 53:5) "But He *was* wounded for our transgressions, *He was* bruised for our iniquities; the chastisement for our peace *was* upon Him, and by His stripes we are healed". It is God's intention that His people walk in and enjoy the full blessings of His Kingdom. God desires to pour out His Spirit upon all flesh and bring life, joy, peace, hope and healing.

The Third Reformation Church will again become a demonstration of this. Paul said in (1 Cor. 4:20) "For the kingdom of God *is* not in word but in power"! (Acts 5:12-16) "And through the hands of the apostles many signs and wonders were done among the people. And they were all with one accord in Solomon's Porch. [13] Yet none of the rest dared join them, but the people esteemed them highly. [14] And believers were increasingly added to the Lord, multitudes of both men and women, [15] so that they brought the sick out into the streets and laid *them* on beds and couches, that at least the shadow of Peter passing by might fall on some of them. [16] Also a multitude gathered from the surrounding cities to Jerusalem, bringing sick people and those who were tormented by unclean spirits, and they were all healed."

- **Revolutionary Generosity** - (Acts 4:32; 34-35) "Now the multitude of those who believed were of one heart and one soul; neither did anyone say that any of the things he possessed was his own, but they had all things in common. [34] Nor was there anyone among them who lacked; for all who were possessors of lands or houses sold them, and brought the proceeds of the things that were sold, [35] and laid *them* at the apostles' feet; and they distributed to each as anyone had need."

These people stood out because God had radically transformed their lives. They became followers of Christ in the truest sense of the word (Acts 11:26), because their behaviour, activity, and speech were like Christ. In other words; they were not characterized by the convenient Christianity of today. They withheld nothing – they gave of themselves and their property. They were concerned about the needs of others and even put them ahead of their own. They seized every opportunity to practically demonstrate God's love. It was this revolutionary and radical generosity that gave credibility and impact to their message.

- **Revolutionary Impact** - (Acts 4:33) "And with great power the apostles gave witness to the resurrection of the Lord Jesus. And great grace was upon them all." The Lord added to the church daily those who were being saved. Believers were increasingly added to the Lord, multitudes of both men and women. Isn't that amazing? God was able to use the lives of His people to bring multitudes to Christ. The lives of the people gave the preaching of the Gospel credibility.

The world needs to see that Jesus is real in us, not just someone we claim to love but don't endeavour to follow, by obeying His commands and treating others as we would want to be treated. The world needs to see that Jesus is not only in the salvation business, but also in the life-transforming business, because our lives are testimonies to it. I believe this would result in more opportunities to share the Gospel and to experience the joy of seeing others come to salvation.

When people see that He's transforming us, they'll listen. Because they won't be concentrating on your lack of credibility, they'll be listening for what Jesus can do for them. Your life is your pulpit…never forget that. People need to see God at work in every area of our lives and living! This is a fundamental emphasis of the Third Reformation Church. Your ministry is wherever you are! The Early Church impacted their culture and society and we are called to do likewise.

What is the Church? The Church is people. It is not the building we meet in, it is the people who meet in the building. The Church is made up of all the people throughout the world and throughout history who have accepted Jesus Christ as their personal Saviour. Is the Church perfect? No. Was the First Century Church perfect? No. Will the Church ever be perfect? Yes, but not until we are all in heaven. The kind of Church Jesus intended was to be something that would bring about change and transformation. God desires for the Church to turn this world upside down and right side up. God's desire for the Church has never changed. Today, in many instances, the Church is not living up to its full potential, it is not the Church that Jesus had in mind; but it can be!

CHAPTER 3: A FULLY REFORMED… FULLY FUNCTIONAL 5-FOLD MINISTRY FOR THE CHURCH TODAY!

The mandate of REFORMATION3 MINISTRIES is to demonstrate and offer training and mentoring programmes seeking to restore a true biblical model for a FULLY FUNCTIONAL 5-FOLD MINISTRY IN THE CHURCH TODAY.

I Kings 18:44
Ephesians 4:11

Just as the "little cloud...like a man's hand" (I Kings 18:44) preceded the flooding rain, the Five-fold Ministry Giftings when functioning according to the blueprint Jesus gave, will, I believe, precede the greatest outpouring of the Holy Spirit in power and authority that the Church has ever known.

For over two thousand years the Church has been limping, weak and partially disabled because of its failure to recognize God's provision for power. We can pray and fast for maturity and unity, but the fact is; that our Father's provision is already revealed in (Eph. 4:11-15).

Those who reject this truth are perhaps motivated by an incorrect understanding of the Five-fold Ministry and the Ministry Gifts. They may feel that the recognition of these gifts would impose some sort of hierarchy upon the Church. This is not true. The function of the Five-fold Ministry Gifts and their benefits are like the benefits of salvation; God doesn't force them on us.

David said, in (Ps. 103:1-5) "Bless the Lord, O my soul; and all that is within me, *bless* His holy name! [2] Bless the Lord, O my soul, and forget not all His benefits", he then goes on to mention the benefits of salvation; healing, deliverance, favour, provision and providence…He made you and He wants to complete you (Phil. 1:6). He has given you benefits, His good will; He is behind you and wants to see "that you may prosper in all things and be in health, just as your soul prospers" (3 John 1:2). The choice is ours, however, to enter into the "deeper" benefits of our salvation. It is the same with the Five-fold Ministry Gifts.

I recall hearing this analogy from a preacher, who used it to describe the condition of today's Church. Before departing on a long trip to assist his family who were relocating to another city, he gave instructions to a friend to make sure the car was ready for the journey. When he arrived, he discovered that the car which was supposed to haul his sister-in-law and her family as well as a trailer had only four of its six cylinders functioning. Additionally, the transmission had only second and third gear... no first or reverse! He said, "We survived the 1300 mile trip. However, our journey would have much easier had the car been functioning the way its designers had intended!"

Like many new Christians, I was encouraged to begin my study of Scripture, with the Gospels, especially the words of Christ. One thing immediately impacted me (even as a relatively new convert) while studying Jesus' teachings, was that He expected His Church to operate in power, unity and maturity. Years later, after 25 years of full-time pastoral ministry, I can only conclude that today's Church is weak and divided because we are running on only one or two cylinders instead of the five originally intended.

The term "Five-fold Ministry" comes from (Eph. 4:11-12) "And He Himself gave some *to be* apostles, some prophets, some evangelists, and some pastors and teachers, [12] for the equipping of the saints for the work of ministry, for the edifying of the body of Christ". Jesus has given these ministry gifts to the Church: Apostles, Prophets, Evangelists, Pastors, and Teachers. If the Church is to be healthy and fulfil its mandate it needs the influence of all five of these gifts. Unfortunately, it is very rare to see this happening today. We need a resurrection of team ministry and a healthy balance of ministry gifts.

Certain Bible expositors teach that some of these ministries were only temporarily given. The Dispensationalists, for example, claim that once the Apostolic Age was over there was no longer any need for **apostles** in the Church. Then there are the Cessasionists who maintain that all 'supernatural gifts' have ceased and no longer operate and therefore reject both the apostolic and prophetic ministries today. There are those who even assert that the ministry of the **evangelist** belongs only to New Testament times. All of the Five-fold Ministry Gifts, however, are, and were always intended by Jesus to be a permanent part of the Church and they are as valid and necessary in every generation, and will be in operation until He returns.

Sometimes, in congregations, one ministry gift is accentuated almost to the exclusion and disregard of the others. In many churches today, the only ministry that is acknowledged is that of the **pastor**. For this reason, it is possibly the most misunderstood and misused ministry title in the church. Many theological seminaries process their students through a pastor-shaped door, and those who graduate, come out shaped into a mould that is not necessarily of God's making. But in our REFORMATION3 COLLEGE OF MINISTRY & LEADERSHIP training programmes, we are committed to enabling our students to discover their Five-fold Ministry and function in it!

Imagine having an **evangelist** as a pastor. They have one primary objective, to get the congregation saved every week! The congregation is not adequately cared for pastorally and they are never discipled to maturity through effective teaching, but they know how to respond to every altar call! Under these ministries, you find the same people at the altar every week; they're locked into cycles of recovery, but they never break through because it's the "truth" that sets people free (John 8:32). "Let the word of Christ dwell in you richly in all wisdom, teaching and admonishing one another in psalms and hymns and spiritual songs, singing with grace in your hearts to the Lord" (Col. 3:16).

If we are going to see a full manifestation of Christ's ministry to the Body, all the five ministries must be operating together. The **Teacher** needs to be inspired by the **Prophet** and the **Prophet** needs to be tempered by the **Pastor**. The **Evangelist** needs the discipline of the **Teacher** and the **Apostle** needs the partnership of all the rest to fulfil the total call of apostleship.

What often happens in some churches is they get over-developed in one area and remain under-developed in others. We have to have balance (1 Cor. 14:40). One church can be known for its teaching and another for its evangelism, but the Lord's purpose is for us to be strong in every area. "All Scripture *is* given by inspiration of God, and *is* profitable for doctrine, for reproof, for correction, for instruction in righteousness, [17] that the man of God may be complete, thoroughly equipped for every good work" (2 Tim. 3:16-17).

In the same way, what does it profit a church if it has a powerful teaching ministry and is established in the Gospel (Col. 2:7), and never applies it (James 1:22), if it never goes and evangelises with it (1 Pet. 3:15)? Equally, what is the point of a church that is passionate about evangelism without ever taking time to learn what the Gospel is and how to disciple those who come to faith? That is why it is necessary for every Christian to come under the ministry of all five of these Ascension Gifts! Where this is not possible within the context of a local church or group of churches, there is great benefit in seeking to establish relationship with an Apostolic Network that can provide this for your ministry and or congregation.

If you look at the illustration of the five fingers...Look at your hand and see the thumb and the fingers. The **Apostle**, as the thumb, moves in authority to govern the Body of Christ. The index finger, which points the way, appropriately pictures the **Prophet** who guides the church by revealing the mind of God. The **Evangelist**, the longest finger, reaches and gathers the people. The **Pastor**, the finger that the wedding band is placed on is "married" to the church. They feed, guard and protect the sheep. The **Teacher**, as the little finger, can get into the ear farther than anyone else to ground and establish believers in the Word of God. We are perfected by the Five-fold Ministry.

The Five-fold Ministry is like a family preparing a meal for dinner: The **Prophet** says: "Stir the pot!" The **Pastor** says: "Let it simmer!" The **Apostle** says: "I'm going hunting for the meat for the stew!" The **Evangelist** says: "Let's go and invite the neighbours!" The **Teacher** says: "I am leading a course in cooking and nutrition." Each ministry has its place and its special purpose so that every aspect of the ministry is covered.

CHAPTER 4: BIBLICAL DEFINITIONS OF THE 5-FOLD ASCENSION GIFTS

We refer to the Five-fold Ministry Gifts as Ascension Gifts because they are gifts given after Christ's ascension into Heaven (Eph. 4:8). Below is a brief description of the Five-fold Ministry Gifts. Keep in mind that these gifts refer to a *person*. With the Nine Manifestation Gifts in (1 Cor. 12) a person may have a gift or operate in a gift; with the Five-fold Ministry Gifts the person is the gift.

APOSTLE: "Governs"

An **Apostle** is "one chosen and sent with a special commission." The twelve apostles chosen by Jesus were witnesses of the resurrection (Acts 4:33) - "And with great power the apostles gave witness to the resurrection of the Lord Jesus. And great grace was upon them all". Elsewhere in the New Testament, other people are also called **"apostles"**, aside from the twelve:

Matthias - selected to replace Judas Iscariot (Acts 1:15-26). **Barnabas** - a missionary "sent out" by the Jerusalem apostles (Acts 11:22, 30; 12:25), later by the Church of Antioch (Acts 13:1-15:39); Luke and Paul explicitly call him an "apostle" (Acts 14:14; 1 Cor. 9:1-6). **Paul** - often calls himself an "apostle" of Jesus, especially in beginning his letters (Rom. 1:1; 1 Cor. 1:1; 2 Cor. 1:1; Gal. 1:1; Eph. 1:1; etc.), or when stressing his equal status with the other apostles (Rom. 11:13; 1 Cor. 9:1-5; 15:7-10; 2 Cor. 12:12; Gal. 1:17-19).

Apollos - never individually called an "apostle," but clearly included when Paul refers to "us apostles" (1 Cor. 4:9; cf. 1:12; 3:4 - 4:6). **Silas and Timothy** - again, not called "apostles" individually, but included when Paul says, "we... as apostles of Christ" (1 Thess. 2:7). **Andronicus and Junia** - a married couple (or brother and sister), "relatives" of Paul, who are "prominent among the apostles" (Rom. 16:7). There were also false apostles and (2 Cor. 11:13-15; Rev. 2:2) warned the churches concerning them.

An **Apostle** will usually be able to operate in most or all of the other Five-fold Offices should the need arise. Their primary gifting lies in the following areas:

- Pioneering new churches (1 Cor. 3:6; 1 Cor. 9:2),
- Grounding the Church in truth (Col. 1:25),
- Preserving unity in the Body (1 Cor. 3:3-5),
- Laying foundations in the Church (1 Cor. 3:10),
- Setting things in order (Titus 1:5),
- Fostering a vision beyond the local church (2 Cor. 8),
- Fathering new ministries (2 Tim. 1:6), and a
- Breakthrough-type ministry of miracles (2 Cor. 12:12).

PROPHET: "Guides"

Prophets have the supernatural endowment to perceive the heart and purpose of God and declare it to people, churches, cities, and nations. **Prophets** receive revelation from the Lord in various ways but the most common is through hearing and seeing. They are also entrusted to equip the people of God to hear the voice of the Lord for themselves and to activate them to move in the supernatural Gifts of the Spirit.

The ministry of the **Prophet** involves being "moved by the Holy Spirit" (2 Pet. 1:21) " For prophecy never came by the will of man, but holy men of God spoke *as they were* moved by the Holy Spirit". This verse does not only relate to the initial revelation of Scripture, but also the ongoing voice of the Lord to His people!

Prophetic utterance can be:

- **PREDICTIVE** (Acts 21:10-11) "And as we stayed many days, a certain prophet named Agabus came down from Judea. [11] When he had come to us, he took Paul's belt, bound his *own* hands and feet, and said, "Thus says the Holy Spirit, 'So shall the Jews at Jerusalem bind the man who owns this belt, and deliver *him* into the hands of the Gentiles.'" (Acts 11:27-28) "And in these days prophets came from Jerusalem to Antioch. [28] Then one of them, named Agabus, stood up and showed by the Spirit that there was going to be a great famine throughout all the world, which also happened in the days of Claudius Caesar".

Agabus was a "prophet from Jerusalem" in the early New Testament era. He is mentioned twice in the Scriptures, both times involving the apostle Paul. The first reference was near the beginning of Paul's Ministry when he was still known as Saul, not long after his conversion. The second reference to Agabus was years later when the well-seasoned apostle Paul was returning from the third of his major missionary journeys. Both times, Agabus prophesied, and both times, because he was a true prophet of God, what he said would happen, happened. This is further evidence that prophets continued to operate after the death and ascension of Christ.

- **DIRECTIVE** (Acts 13:1-3) "Now in the church that was at Antioch there were certain prophets and teachers: Barnabas, Simeon who was called Niger, Lucius of Cyrene, Manaen who had been brought up with Herod the tetrarch, and Saul. [2] As they ministered to the Lord and fasted, the Holy Spirit said, "Now separate to Me Barnabas and Saul for the work to which I have called them." [3] Then, having fasted and prayed, and laid hands on them, they sent *them* away." Further proof of the operation of prophets in the New Testament Church and their accepted role.

- **CORRECTIVE** (Acts 15:22-23; 27; 32) "Then it pleased the apostles and elders, with the whole church, to send chosen men of their own company to Antioch with Paul and Barnabas, *namely,* Judas who was also named Barsabas, and Silas, leading men among the brethren. [23] They wrote this *letter* by them: The apostles, the elders, and the brethren, To the brethren who are of the Gentiles in Antioch, Syria, and Cilicia: Greetings. [27] We have therefore sent Judas and Silas, who will also report the same things by word of mouth. ³² Now Judas and Silas, themselves being prophets also, exhorted and strengthened the brethren with many words." That corrective word was to keep themselves pure and uncontaminated in terms of doctrine and holiness.

There is such a thing, however, as a false prophet (1 John 4:1) "Beloved, do not believe every spirit, but test the spirits, whether they are of God; because many false prophets have gone out into the world" and so God sets clear guidelines:

- Prophecies should be **TIME-TESTED** (Acts 11:28)…What Agabus prophesied about the great famine, happened.
- The words of a prophet are **JUDGED BY CHURCH LEADERSHIP** (1 Cor. 14:29) "Let two or three prophets speak, and let the others judge".
- Any prophecy should be **CONFIRMED INDEPENDENTLY** (2 Cor. 13:1) "By the mouth of two or three witnesses every word shall be established".
- Any prophecy should **LINE UP WITH SCRIPTURE**, "the more sure word of prophecy" (2 Pet. 1:19).

The **Prophet** operates best in teamwork with the **Apostle** (for example; Paul and Silas). A **Prophet** is not just someone with a prophetic anointing, but a recognised ministry to the Body at large.

THREE LEVELS OF THE PROPHETIC:

Prophecy is like a swimming pool. There is a shallow end that all can safely use. This is inspirational prophecy or the **GIFT OF PROPHECY** where our aim is to encourage, build up and comfort people. It is non-directive, not correctional and seeks to bless people and glorify the Lord. When Paul declared that he desired that all would prophesy (1 Cor. 14:1; 5) it was this level of prophecy he had in mind. It was not a general call for everyone to become a **Prophet**.

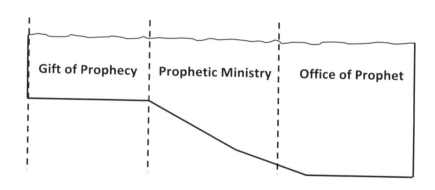

After the shallow end, there is a middle section, where the water gets progressively deeper. Here we move into the area of **PROPHETIC MINISTRY:** Prophetic Ministry is quite different from the Gift of Prophecy. Many people will experience prophecy as a one-off gift for a particular time or purpose. Prophetic Ministry is concerned with the church. It is concerned with the direction we take and how we will get to our destination. Every church has times of testing, battles to fight and things to overcome. The **Prophetic Ministry**

brings God's perspective, releases vision and calling and undermines the enemy. It is concerned with seeing the church fulfilling its call. It focuses on the supremacy of God in times of trouble. It has one hand in the past and one in the future and is able to bring both elements into the present to help us make sense of what we are going through. This prophetic perspective ignites faith and hope and gives us the energy to fight on and break through.

THE OFFICE OF A PROPHET: For a person to stand in the **Office of a Prophet,** they would need to be called to the Five-fold Ministry and recognised as such. The **Office of a Prophet** moves deeper into the supernatural realm of hearing God and being His mouthpiece. The **Prophet** is concerned with holiness and purity and seeks to prepare the Bride of Christ, literally making ready a people prepared for the Lord. Their message is to churches, cities, regions and nations. Their words will often be accompanied by miracles and clear signs of the supernatural presence of God. Their words will invest the church with supernatural faith as they both forth-tell the word of the Lord and foretell His purposes.

It is my conviction, that only someone standing in the **Office of Prophet** should exercise the authority of predictive, directive and corrective prophecy, and even then only within clear structures of accountability and protective guidelines. **Prophets** act as catalysts and activists within the church in that their words often "go before" and open up the way. God still reveals His secrets to His servants the **prophets**!

Ironically, one of the most important roles of the **New Testament Prophet** is not to prophesy, but to train and activate people to hear the Lord for themselves. Secondly, to teach believers how to find and follow the will of God for themselves. Thirdly, it is to train and mentor people in the gift and ministry of prophecy and to help churches establish the right framework and protocols for it. Fourthly, it is to bring the Word of the Lord either in inspired preaching or by supernatural prophetic utterance. This is not necessarily the order; it depends on the context or circumstance and the gifting of the **Prophet**.

<u>EVANGELIST</u>: "Gathers"

More than any other Five-fold gifting, the **Evangelist,** is intent on reaching the lost. **Evangelists** make the primary aim of their ministry to see the unsaved come to salvation. There gifting operates in diverse ways, whether by preaching or personal association. Perhaps their greatest mandate, though, is to equip and activate the Church to evangelize, both corporately and individually.

Evangelists extend the frontiers of God's Kingdom. Good examples are the ministry of Stephen and Philip:

(Acts 6:3-7) "Therefore, brethren, seek out from among you seven men of *good* reputation, full of the Holy Spirit and wisdom, whom we may appoint over this business; [4] but we will give ourselves continually to prayer and to the ministry of the word." [5] And the saying pleased the whole multitude. And they chose Stephen, a man full of faith and the Holy Spirit, and Philip...[6] whom they set before the apostles; and when they had prayed, they laid hands on them.[7] Then the word of God spread, and the number of the disciples multiplied greatly in Jerusalem, and a great many of the priests were obedient to the faith."

(Acts 8:5-7) "Then Philip went down to the city of Samaria and preached Christ to them. [6] And the multitudes with one accord heeded the things spoken by Philip, hearing and seeing the miracles which he did.[7] For unclean spirits, crying with a loud voice, came out of many who were possessed; and many who were paralyzed and lame were healed. [8] And there was great joy in that city."

Evangelists work in close partnership with the apostolic ministry. In (2 Tim. 4:5) Paul, the apostle tells Timothy, "But you be watchful in all things, endure afflictions, do the work of an evangelist, fulfil your ministry."

(1 Thess. 3:2) "And sent Timothy, our brother and minister of God, and our fellow labourer in the Gospel of Christ, to establish you and encourage you concerning your faith."

PASTOR: "Guards"

The **Pastor**, more than the others, is focused on the flock. The **Pastor** has a relational ministry that is connected to a group of believers. The **Pastor** oversees, provides spiritual care, healing, and correction when needed. They are portrayed in Scripture as shepherds and that sums up the true nature of their calling - they love the people of God and want to see them living in the destiny that God has for them. I have observed that many people who carry the title **"Pastor"** are not really pastors, but one of the other ministry gifts. If this is the case, the congregation will not flourish unless someone else in leadership is fulfilling the pastoral role.

The Greek word for **pastor**, "poimen", means "one who tends sheep or cares for flocks" (John 21:15-17). But this word is used only in (Eph. 4:11). Elsewhere in the New Testament, other words are used: "shepherd", "elder" and "overseer". This is significant, so a comparison of these ministries should be made.

A Five-fold ministry **Pastor** is not simply a leader over a local church, but has a Body-wide expression of ministry. They are more accurately a "pastor of pastors" or "lead/senior pastor" or a "pastor of elders" beyond the local body. A **Pastor's** emphasis in ministry is in relationship networking.

- **The Ministry of an Elder:**

It is important here, to clarify the role of elders, because it is not a title but a function. I mention this, because there is widespread error and misinterpretation of this ministry. An elder is simply someone older/more mature in the faith - a "father or mother in the Lord". An elder is not a particular type of ministry, but rather is a leader in the Body.

(1 Pet. 5:1-2) "The elders who are among you I exhort, I who am a fellow elder and a witness of the sufferings of Christ, and also a partaker of the glory that will be revealed: [2] Shepherd the flock of

God which is among you, serving as overseers, not by compulsion but willingly, not for dishonest gain but eagerly".

(Acts 20:17:28) "From Miletus he sent to Ephesus and called for the elders of the church. [18] And when they had come to him, he said to them: "You know, from the first day that I came to Asia, in what manner I always lived among you, [28] Therefore take heed to yourselves and to all the flock, among which the Holy Spirit has made you overseers, to shepherd the church of God which He purchased with His own blood. "

The word "elder" - "presbuteros" - refers to any leadership ministry. An elder may be one of the five or an "overseer" - "episkopos" - over a local church. But whether a person is a **pastor** (one of the Five-fold ministry) or an overseeing elder (in charge of a local Body), both are called to be shepherds.

Following the example of the Chief Shepherd (John 10:1-16), a shepherd's ministry is to feed (verse 9); protect (verse 12), guide (verses 3-4) and love (verse 15) the sheep.

- **The Ministry of a Deacon**:

The first reference to a deacon in the local congregation is found in (Phil. 1:1), where Paul says, "To all the saints in Christ Jesus who are in Philippi, with the bishops (namely elders or spiritual leaders) and deacons". While the New Testament never specifically defines the responsibilities or duties of deacons, what is clear is that it was not a title but a function, and that was primarily to serve in the area of practical ministries; in other words; to provide logistical and material support, so that the spiritual leaders can focus on the Word of God and prayer.

Deacon ministries, ministries of service, hospitality and helps are crucial in the church today. Paul explains the qualities of a deacon in (1 Tim. 3:8-13). Like elders, the New Testament indicates that both men and women were appointed as deacons in the Early Church. In (Rom. 16:1), Paul calls Phoebe a deaconess.

TEACHER: "Grounds"

A **Teacher** is not just someone who teaches. We are all encouraged to teach (Col. 3:16) "Let the word of Christ dwell in you richly in all wisdom, teaching and admonishing one another in psalms and hymns and spiritual songs, singing with grace in your hearts to the Lord". The **Teacher**, however, is a ministry who brings instruction to the Body at large. (Acts 2) says of the New Testament believers, that they "continued in the Apostle's teaching". The **Teacher**, more than the others, is focused on the written Word of God (or the "logos").

Teachers have a great love for the Scriptures and are concerned that the people of God become grounded in the Word. They have the ability to communicate the Word in ways that people understand and they cause others to hunger for the Word. The **Teacher** and the **Prophet** bring a great balance to each other, as we need to be both grounded in the Bible and open to the voice of the Holy Spirit.

Just as we are warned in Scripture concerning false apostles and prophets so also are we cautioned about false teachers and given biblical evidence whereby to access them. "But there were also false prophets among the people, even as there will be false teachers among you, who will secretly bring in destructive heresies, even denying the Lord who bought them, *and* bring on themselves swift destruction. [2] And many will follow their destructive ways, because of whom the way of truth will be blasphemed. [3] By covetousness they will exploit you with deceptive words; for a long time their judgment has not been idle, and their destruction does not slumber" (2 Pet. 2:1-3).

We must seek God for a true restoration of all the Five-fold Ministry Gifts operating together and for team ministry to once more be the norm in the Church. The result will be powerful!

What is the fruit of the **Five-fold Ministry Gifts** functioning properly in the Church? "The equipping of the saints for the work of ministry, for the edifying of the body of Christ, [13] till we all come to the unity of the faith and of the knowledge of the Son of God, to a perfect man, to the measure of the stature of the fullness of Christ; [14] that we should no longer be children, tossed to and fro and carried about with every wind of doctrine, by the trickery of men, in the cunning craftiness of deceitful plotting, [15] but, speaking the truth in love, may grow up in all things into Him who is the head - Christ - [16] from whom the whole body, joined and knit together by what every joint supplies, according to the effective working by which every part does its share, causes growth of the body for the edifying of itself in love (Eph. 4:12-16).

- **(Verse 11) - THE FIVE-FOLD MINISTRIES:** These are not titles but ministry functions. There is nothing "elevated" about these gifts. They simply have a special purpose.

- **(Verse 12) - THE FUNCTION:** "...to prepare God's people for works of service, so that the body of Christ may be built up." These five leadership gifts were not simply given to do the work of the ministry but to enable God's people to do the work of the ministry.

- **(Verse 13) - THE TIME-FRAME:** "...till we all come to the unity of the faith and of the knowledge of the Son of God, to a perfect man, to the measure of the stature of the fullness of Christ". The Five-fold Ministry did not pass away at the end of the first century, but was given until the maturing of the Body in unity, knowledge and expression of Christ's fullness.

It is important to state that the Five-fold Ministry are not self-commissioned, "And He Himself gave some..." neither are they simply the designated leaders of a church. In Scripture they are clearly defined ministries that have an impact on the Church as a whole. Biblically, their scope of ministry is broader than just a local church. There are two pre-requisites for a Five-fold Ministry Gift to be established; firstly, there needs to be recognition by the wider Body and secondly, their ministry needs to be received and be operational within the wider Body.

A person may potentially have a Five-fold Ministry Gift, prior to the endorsement of these; however, they will not yet be operating in the entire expression and authority of that gift. Only when the Five-fold Ministries of (Eph. 4:11) begin functioning as God intended - both as individual ministries and as Apostolic Teams - will the full advantage of their combined anointing be actualized.

CHAPTER 5: REFORMATION OF THE FIVE-FOLD MINISTRY "TEAM"

The Book of Acts speaks of a time when all things will be restored (Acts 3:20-21) "...and that He may send Jesus Christ, who was preached to you before, [21] whom heaven must receive until the times of restoration of all things, which God has spoken by the mouth of all His holy prophets since the world began."

Much of the spiritual life of the Church was lost during the Dark Ages (500-1500 AD). Often the gifts and ministries of Christ and of the Holy Spirit were replaced with organizational structures which maintained a form of the real thing but had lost the power. Restoration began with the Protestant Reformation (1517-1600) and built truth upon truth over the years. Often, as history records, each successive restoration movement was persecuted by the previous group. Over the last few decades we have seen the restoration or re-emphasis of each of the Five-fold Ministry Gifts:

- **1950's - Evangelist accompanied by healings, deliverance and widespread evangelism**
- **1960's - Pastor seen develop through emphasis on "Body life" and the Charismatic Renewal**

- 1970's - Teacher growing with teaching conferences and the Faith Teaching Movement
- 1980's - Prophet with a strong prophetic movement and many prophetic conferences
- 1990's - Apostles with the Apostolic Movement recognising the 5-FOLD MINISTRIES
- 2000's - Saints Movement and now recognition of APOSTOLIC TEAMS!

We have witnessed the singular restoration of the **apostle, prophet, evangelist, pastor** and **teacher**, as individual giftings, we have not, however, experienced the power of the apostolic dimension released, as in the Book of Acts (Acts 4:33; 19:11-12), or the prophetic voice that can literally shut the heavens and stop the rain (1 Kings 17:1; James 5:17-18). There has been an "emphasis" on each one. They have been endeavouring to define their function, place and level of authority within the local and broader Church but as fingers on a hand, they must learn to balance one another, compliment and work alongside each other; in order to get the task done. God is, in this reformation, beginning to bring from the nations of the earth the **apostles, prophets, evangelists, pastors** and **teachers** to join forces together and become one voice, one mighty hand of power!

I am convinced that this was always the purpose and intention of Jesus, when He gave these gifts. They functioned together in His person and ministry and I believe they were never designed to operate independently and separately. This is one of the main features of this Third Reformation. This is the key to unlock what each of the restorational moves has been leading the Church toward. This is the key to open up for the Church a whole new dimension of revelation, relevance and renewal. We will see the impact of these ministries as they work together to equip the Body of Christ and bring forth an apostolic people. The Church will rise up with people empowered and equipped by the Holy Spirit ready to meet the challenges of the times and the days in which we are living.

We need to be prepared for the emergence and formulation of fresh expressions of apostolically-based church structures and leadership styles; that the Holy Spirit will facilitate to express His purpose and priority in this hour. Apostolic Overseers will encourage, cultivate and lead local church apostolic teams that will, in turn, advance the people of God to step into the manifestation of the apostolic anointing that is being released on us all!

HOW YOUR MINISTRY RELATES TO THE FIVE-FOLD MINISTRY:

Every believer needs to be connected to ALL of the Five-fold Ministries in order to come to maturity. A believer, who assumes he or she can operate on their own, will never experience the full measure of the calling that God intended for them.

Some claim that these gifts are given equally throughout the entire Body of Christ so that everyone is gifted as an **apostle, prophet, evangelist**, **pastor** or **teacher**. But, Scripture is clear that these are special ministries given to some and not all the Church. They are leadership functions not given TO everyone but they are given FOR everyone. They are 'ENABLING' MINISTRIES that equip and activate

God's people for the ministry. Therefore, I believe we can see them as 'UMBRELLA' MINISTRIES under which the various ministries and giftings "cluster" according to the basic nature of their calling and function; for activation, accountability and access to mentoring.

The **Apostle**, as well as working with those in Church Government (elders and prophets), would have the responsibility of mentoring those with the 'power gifts' - faith, healing and miracles. Those with Gifts of Administration (deacons and administrators), would naturally work alongside those in church government. The **Prophet** would be mentoring those with the Inspirational or Vocal Gifts - Gift of Prophecy, Tongues and Interpretation of Tongues. Those with the Gifts of Revelation, Words of Wisdom, Knowledge and Discerning of Spirits would also benefit from prophetic mentoring.

The **Evangelist**, those called to the Five-fold Ministry, need the support of the prophetic and apostolic office as they develop and step out, as well as motivating, training and activating the whole church to outreach, evangelism and missions - local, national and international. (Acts 1:8) "But you shall receive power when the Holy Spirit has come upon you; and you shall be witnesses to Me in Jerusalem, and in all Judea and Samaria, and to the end of the earth". The **Pastor** would be a very natural mentor for those gifts that fall into the category of 'helps or service' and the pastoral ministries. The **Teacher** would be mentoring the teaching, training and discipling ministries.

The undergirding of this Third Reformation, though, lies in the revelation and re-implementation of the New Testament dynamic, that every area of ministry needs not only to be connected to the relevant Five-fold Ministry Gift/Person, but every area of ministry, in order to function fully, needs to have an apostolic, prophetic, evangelistic, pastoral and teaching/discipling dimension to it.

For instance the **Worship Ministry** - Needs the **apostolic** dimension, to break through, touch heaven and release the supernatural dimension of God's glory. It needs to be **prophetic** and "forth-tell" the greatness, glory and power of God. It needs to activate and release the vocal/utterance gifts and the "Song of the Lord" (1 Cor. 14:15). It needs an **evangelistic** dynamic to be able to draw in those who are not yet saved, so they can encounter the Father in worship, through songs of redemption and the cross. He said that "And I, if I am lifted up from the earth, will draw all *peoples* to Myself" (John 12:32). Cross-centered worship is as important as cross-centered preaching.

It needs a **pastoral** dimension in that worship has to include sensitivity to the journey that people are on and facilitate a deepening and growing of their intimacy with God. It also has a **teaching** element. Our worship has to be in "spirit and truth" (John 4:24). Much of the psalms that were recited and sung, were about remembering and establishing biblical truth; and by hearing that, to believe and have faith. "So then faith *comes* by hearing, and hearing by the word of God" (Rom. 10:17).

I absolutely believe that every area of gifting and ministry in the Church, if it is truly going to be apostolic - an extension of the ministry of Christ, must contain EVERY ONE of these elements.

Obviously some will be more pronounced than others depending on the specific gift or ministry, but they will nevertheless be there. This will complete and add to the overall effectiveness and contribution of these ministries in and to the local church on an unprecedented scale. It will transform churches and release anointing, power and fruit/results, never experienced before!

CHAPTER 6: REFORMING MINISTRY - RECLAIMING THE NEW TESTAMENT PATTERN

THE MINISTRY OF CHRIST:

It is important to establish at the outset, that all ministry is ultimately the ministry of Christ being expressed through the believer by the anointing of the Holy Spirit. We are His Body on the earth and our primary purpose, as such, is to continue His work (Rom. 12:3-5; 1 Cor. 12:12-26; Eph. 1:18-23; 2:19-22; 5:25-32; Col. 1:17-20; 3:14-16). Jesus exercised all the Five-fold ministries while He was on the earth. He is our **APOSTLE** (Heb. 3:1) refers to Jesus as the Apostle and High Priest of our confession, **PROPHET** (Luke 24:19) Luke calls Jesus a Prophet mighty in deed and word before God and all the people, **EVANGELIST** (Matt. 9:35) Jesus travelled from place to place preaching the Gospel of the Kingdom, **PASTOR** (1 Pet. 5:2-4) speaks of Jesus as the Chief Shepherd, and **TEACHER** (John 3:2) Nicodemus refers to Jesus as Rabbi and teacher. Every ministry, including that of the Five-fold Ministry is an extension of the ministry of Christ Himself.

THE NEW TESTAMENT PATTERN - EVERY MEMBER A MINISTER:

One of the greatest needs of the Church today is to return to the New Testament model of ministry. Looking back to the 16th Century we see that it was a time of reformation for the Church. God enabled His people to rediscover the true essence of the Gospel, the fact that we are saved by grace alone, through faith alone, in Christ alone! "For by grace you have been saved through faith, and that not of yourselves; *it is* the gift of God, [9] not of works, lest anyone should boast" (Eph. 2:8-9).

The Reformers, such as Martin Luther and John Calvin, rediscovered the biblical teaching of 'the priesthood of all believers', namely, that every believer has equal access to the presence of God. We come to the Father through faith in the finished work of Christ on the cross "being justified freely by His grace through the redemption that is in Christ Jesus, [25] whom God set forth *as* a propitiation by His blood, through faith, to demonstrate His righteousness, because in His forbearance God had passed over the sins that were previously committed" (Rom. 3:24-25).

By His grace, we do not require an intervention by a special class of clergy or priests but we can each come boldly to the Throne of Grace through the blood of Jesus. "Therefore, brethren, having boldness to enter the Holiest by the blood of Jesus, [20] by a new and living way which He consecrated for us, through the veil, that is, His flesh, [21] and *having* a High Priest over the house of God, [22] let us draw near with a true heart in full assurance of faith, having our hearts sprinkled from an evil conscience and our bodies washed with pure water" (Heb. 10:19-22). We have the same direct access to God that Jesus has. In other words, He has made us a royal priesthood, a holy nation " But you *are* a chosen generation, a royal priesthood, a holy nation, His own special people, that you may proclaim the praises of Him who called you out of darkness into His marvellous light" (1 Pet. 2:9).

God has chosen us to become His ministers, His priests, and we have been called to serve Him. We come before Him in worship, adoration and prayer, but as priests, we are also called to represent Him in the world. Whatever our job or profession, we are called to spread the fragrance of Christ (2 Cor. 2:14). It also means that we are commissioned to preach the Gospel, teach the Word of God, to heal the sick, to cast out demons - in other words, to do the work of Christ. "Most assuredly, I say to you, he who believes in Me, the works that I do he will do also; and greater *works* than these he will do, because I go to My Father" (John 14:12). "So Jesus said to them again, "Peace to you! As the Father has sent Me, I also send you" (John 20:21).

The moment we are born-again we become His "ministers of reconciliation" (2 Cor. 5:17-18) "Therefore, if anyone *is* in Christ, *he is* a new creation; old things have passed away; behold, all things have become new. [18] Now all things *are* of God, who has reconciled us to Himself through Jesus Christ, and has given us the ministry of reconciliation". We have all, according to (2 Thess. 2:13-14), been called, "But we are bound to give thanks to God always for you, brethren beloved by the Lord, because God from the beginning chose you for salvation through sanctification by the Spirit and belief in the truth, [14] to which He called you by our gospel, for the obtaining of the glory of our Lord Jesus Christ".

A minister is anyone who serves. The definition of ministry, therefore, is service. Everyone can minister; what's more everyone has been commanded by God to minister, because we all are called to be servants. Paul said, "I, therefore, the prisoner of the Lord, beseech you to walk worthy of the calling with which you were called, [2] with all lowliness and gentleness, with longsuffering, bearing with one another in love, [3] endeavoring to keep the unity of the Spirit in the bond of peace. [4] *There is* one body and one Spirit, just as you were called in one hope of your calling; [5] one Lord, one faith, one baptism; [6] one God and Father of all, who *is* above all, and through all, and in you all. [7] But to each one of us grace was given according to the measure of Christ's gift" (Eph. 4:1-7).

So according to the New Testament pattern, every believer is:

- Created for ministry (Eph. 2:10)

- Saved for ministry (2 Tim. 1:9)

- Called to ministry (1 Pet. 2:9-10)

- Gifted for ministry (1 Pet. 4:10)

- Authorized for ministry (Matt. 28:18-20)

- Commanded to minister (Matt. 20:26-28)

- Needed for ministry (1 Cor. 12:27)

- Accountable for ministry (Matt. 25:14-30)

- Rewarded for ministry (Col. 3:23-24)

The results of the Second Reformation are still with us today, but the full revelation of the priesthood of all believers has somehow been lost through centuries of church traditions and denominational institutionalism. The consequence is that today, the vast majority of believers do not think of themselves as ministers; they understand that to be the job of the full-time, paid staff of the church. We still have this unbiblical distinction between the so-called 'laity' and the 'clergy'... between them: the 'holy ones', the 'anointed ones', the 'gifted' ones, and us: the 'ordinary' Christians.

We need a new reformation, arising from a paradigm shift and a fresh revelation about the Body of Christ. To embrace the fact that we are all called, chosen and anointed by God to serve Him; that He gives us all gifts and calls us all to the ministry of reconciliation (2 Cor. 5:11-21). Our local churches will never be successful in fulfilling their corporate vision until we grasp this and put (Eph. 4:11-16) into practice. Yet very few churches actually function like that. The concept of part-time Christians led by professional clergy is totally foreign to Scripture. The Bible is clear - we are all in the ministry together!

SO, WHERE DO YOU FIND YOUR PLACE?

To be ignorant of or to neglect your gift is to belittle the value and significance that God has placed on your life. The fact is that God ordained you, from the foundation of the earth, for such a time as this, and specifically allocated you your place in the Body of Christ. "But now God has set the members, each one of them, in the body just as He pleased" (1 Cor. 12:18).

We are all called to be participators, but it is not always evident as to where our gifting lies. Even when a gifting is evident, there must be a willingness to be trained and mentored. Training time is never wasted. Athletes often train for years for a major competition or medal. And all of us are commanded to run so as to win the race.

Teamwork was a vital part of the Early Church mission, strategy and service. As leaders with governmental authority seek to lead the church into this new reformation, familiar patterns and styles of church life may change. This will mean that every person will need to accommodate a church structure and dynamic based upon New Testament and therefore Divine precedent, being willing to relinquish tradition and prejudice. As the Church submits to this process, Jesus will be building His Body. As the ministry gifts operate, people in the church Body will mature in their understanding of their personal role, and that of others.

There are twenty-one Gifts given to the Church and these may be grouped into five main categories. This helps us to understand their importance and contribution to Body life and ministry. You can find more information as well as facilities to help you discover and activate your gifts and ministries on our website: www.reformation3.com

1. NINE GIFTS OF THE SPIRIT:

- Three Gifts of **Revelation**: Word of Wisdom, Word of Knowledge and Discerning of Spirits.
- Three Gifts of **Power**: Faith, Healing and Miracles.
- Three Gifts of **Inspiration,** also known as the Vocal Gifts: Prophecy, Tongues and Interpretation of Tongues.

In (1 Cor. 12:1-11), three Greek words define these gifts: (1.) "Pneumatikos", (v.1), (2.) "charismata", (v.4), and (3.) "phaneros", (v.7). These refer to spiritual power tools (v.1), gifts of grace, (v.4), and manifestations of the Spirit (v.7). These gifts are endowments and not rewards. They are unrelated to personal merit, but are supernatural tools imparted to the believer to fulfill a function in the Body. The giver is the Holy Spirit, the recipient; any believer, received by grace through faith. One may desire and pray to receive these gifts, although not necessarily operate in more than one of them. Through these endowments of supernatural ability, the Holy Spirit works through the believer to accomplish the mission of the Church.

2. GIFTS OF RULE, LEADERSHIP OR GOVERNMENT: Greek - "Roistemi"

This includes Apostle, Prophet and Elders. God calls and appoints individuals to exercise government in the Church Body. The Five-fold ministry gifts of Prophet and Apostle, MAY operate in church government, but a person in one of these offices is NOT automatically a part of their local church government. Likewise, elders are not always a part of the Five-fold ministry.

In the New Testament church, the apostles discerned whom to appoint to church government through fasting, prayer, and the laying on of hands. It was always a supernatural process, never a democratic one. The Greek terms used for governmental gifts include: (1.) "Presbuteros" (or elders), with an emphasis on a tested character. (2.) "Episkopos", a bishop, overseer or supervisor, with the duty to superintend the church. This was a functional role, not intended as a title or badge of office. (3.) "Proistemi", as one who leads by example as of a shepherd who goes before the flock. (4.) "Hegeomai", emphasizing accountability to God. (Heb. 13:7; 17). (5.) "Poimaino", as a shepherd, one who tends or cares. Elders are appointed by apostles, prophets and presbyters. They exist in plurality, and are of recognized character. They are accountable to God for the care of the believers.

3. GIFTS OF ADMINISTRATION: Greek - "Kubernesis"

Administrators and deacons are in this category. These are essential participants in local Body life as well as on mission. They are accounted among other giftings of high value, being listed by Paul, together with apostles, prophets, teachers and miracle workers. (1 Cor. 12:28). "Kubernesis" is a marine term describing one who guides a vessel to a pre-determined destination. The course is set by church government, but faithfully pursued by church administrators.

New Testament administrators were required to be deeply spiritual people, whose voluntary undertaking of the practical aspects of church ministry, released others to attend to their primary gifting (Acts 6: 2-4).

4. GIFTS OF SERVICE OR HELPS: Greek - "Antilepsis"

In this category fall the Gifts of Helps, Mercy and Giving. This is a ministry of mercy and compassion, often to the outcast and broken. "Antilepsis" means to hold someone up, or bear them up, as in supporting them. In (Matt. 25: 31-46), it is clear that the ministry of helps is close to the heart of Jesus, "[35] for I was hungry and you gave Me food; I was thirsty and you gave Me drink; I was a stranger and you took Me in; [36] I *was* naked and you clothed Me; I was sick and you visited Me; I was in prison and you came to Me". To exercise the gift of service is to assume any number of compassionate, practical ministries, within and without the church Body.

5. ASCENSION GIFTS OR FIVE-FOLD MINISTRY GIFTS: Greek - "Dorea" and "Doma"

As stated previously, these gifts are people, given to serve the Body of Christ, called and appointed of God and are the Apostle, Prophet,

Evangelist, Pastor and Teacher. The Greek words emphasize the supernatural dimensions of the gift which are an extension of Jesus within His Church. These gifts are not redundant until the Church has reached the fullness of the stature of Jesus and becomes His embodiment on earth in substance and impact. The gifts are the tools of the Master Builder, and essential to the divine blueprint to:

- Reach the world with the Gospel of Salvation and the Message of the Kingdom.

- To practically demonstrate the principles and values of the Kingdom of Heaven on earth, and thereby provide an authentic and visible alternative to world culture, taking dominion over all counter-kingdom culture, in all the key areas of societal influence; namely the 'Seven Mountains'.

WHAT IT MEANS TO BE EQUIPPED: Greek - "Katartzo"

The biblical mandate and function of the Five-fold Ministry leaders is to prepare God's people for their ministry, so that 'the body of Christ may be built up...' The New Testament Greek word translated as 'prepare', or 'equip' is "katartidzo", which has a powerful application. A fuller interpretation of this word enables us to grasp more comprehensively the way that God uses leadership to train and empower us to effectively be able to serve Him and to be His representatives to the world. "Now then, we are ambassadors for Christ, as though God were pleading through us: we implore *you* on Christ's behalf, be reconciled to God" (2 Cor. 5:20).

God continues to prepare us throughout our lives. Therefore we should never feel that we have to wait until we're "good enough". God will use you as long as you are willing and remain teachable. So begin now…don't wait until you think you've arrived! Ministry is "service", so begin by finding a place where you can serve and roll up your sleeves and get on with it. In our ministry we will never appoint anyone to a leadership or ministry function, who does not first demonstrate a servant heart or attitude.

When the Ascension Gifts operate properly and are accepted by the Church, the consequence is that God's people are prepared for service and for His work in the world. The Body of Christ can then be released for the ministry of Christ. The leaders and members begin to work together to get the job done.

- **Being restored**: "Katartidzo" means 'to restore something to its former condition' or 'to make something right again' (Gal. 6:1) "Brethren, if a man is overtaken in any trespass, you who *are* spiritual restore such a one in a spirit of gentleness, considering yourself lest you also be tempted". If a bone has been broken it needs to be set and to heal before it can be used. In the same way, the Five-fold Ministry are called by God to restore you and make you a useful member in the Body of Christ.

- **Made complete**: "Katartidzo" also means 'to fully equip' - like a ship ready to sail, or a fully trained army totally kitted out and ready for battle. It also means 'to furnish completely'. Unless it is furnished, a house is not complete. Only then, can we move in to live there and enjoy it. That is how God works in you. The Five-fold Ministry is what He has provided, to make you complete as a Christian so that you will be ready to step into His purpose and destiny for your life "Now may the God of peace who brought up our Lord Jesus from the dead, that great Shepherd of the sheep, through the blood of the everlasting covenant, [21] make you complete in every good work to do His will, working in you what is well pleasing in His sight, through Jesus Christ, to whom *be* glory forever and ever. Amen" (Heb. 13:20-21).

- **Fully trained**: "Katartidzo" was also used in the context of 'training apprentices' or 'disciplining children'. God wants to train us so that we will be skilled and disciplined in His work. "A disciple is not above his teacher, but everyone who is perfectly trained will be like his teacher" (Luke 6:40).

- **Prepared and made ready**: Finally, "katartidzo" means 'to prepare in advance' so that when the opportunity arises, everything is in place. God's will is for you to be ready and equipped, with your life in order, so that you can fully represent Him in any situation. "For we are His workmanship, created in Christ Jesus for good works, which God prepared beforehand that we should walk in them" (Eph. 2:10).

HOW TO RECOGNISE YOUR MINISTRY:

- **Your relationship with God** - Your ministry will always flow out of your relationship with God - He must always take first place. Seek Him for what ministry He has or wants to give you - expect Him to speak and listen for His response. "My sheep hear My voice, and know them, and they follow Me" (John 10:27). "For we are His workmanship, created in Christ Jesus for good works, which God prepared beforehand that we should walk in them" (Eph. 2:10).

- **Your character** - This is as important as your ministry - perhaps it is time to allow God to give you a Godly lifestyle - Sin will stop you hearing fully what God is saying, the only way to deal with sin is to repent. "If we say that we have no sin, we deceive ourselves, and the truth is not in us. [9] If we confess our sins, He is faithful and just to forgive us *our* sins and to cleanse us from all unrighteousness" (1 John 1:8-9).

- **Your natural gifting** - This will sometimes be used by God, but it always needs to be surrendered to Him, because He wants to supernaturally empower you. Don't be limited by your natural abilities or lack of them; oftentimes God will use us in areas where in the natural we are weak, and supernaturally equips us in order that we depend totally on Him. "For it is God who works in you both to will and to do for *His* good pleasure" (Phil. 2:13). "Now to Him who is able to do exceedingly abundantly above all that we ask or think, according to the power that works in us" (Eph. 3:20). There is also benefit in participating in a ministry assessment exercise or training/activation programme.

- **Your circumstances** - You should never allow your circumstances in life to limit you; neither the experiences, failures nor the disappointments of the past. The past is something we have to deal with in an appropriate way and then move on. " Brethren, I do not count myself to have apprehended; but one thing *I do,* forgetting those things which are behind and reaching forward to those things which are ahead, [14] I press toward the goal for the prize of the upward call of God in Christ Jesus" (Phil. 3:13-14).

God wants to bring healing, restoration and breakthrough in whatever area is preventing you from moving into and recognising that you should have a ministry. Many people have become disempowered because they have been put down by others, or put themselves down, but God wants to raise you up (Ps. 3:3; 40:2) - we serve a great God, "And raised *us* up together, and made *us* sit together in the heavenly *places* in Christ Jesus" (Eph. 2:6).

- **Your prayer support** - Ask others who you trust in the Body of Christ to pray with you, "Praying always with all prayer and supplication in the Spirit, being watchful to this end with all perseverance and supplication for all the saints" (Eph.6:18). "Confess *your* trespasses to one another, and pray for one another, that you may be healed. The effective, fervent prayer of a righteous man avails much" (James 5:16).

- **Your study of the Word** - Expect Him to speak to you through His Word. Your ministry needs to be on a solid biblical foundation. The Holy Spirit may give you a specific "rhema" word. "But He answered and said, "It is written, 'Man shall not live by bread alone, but by every word that proceeds from the mouth of God" (Matt. 4:4).

- **Your relationships with others** - Expect Him to speak through others especially those you trust and who know you. Sometimes when people are sharing or ministering the Word of God something may "light up" for you, "Your word *is* a lamp to my feet and a light to my path" (Ps. 119:105).

- **Your prophetic words** - There are times when God gives specific prophecies for you. If God speaks directionally through a prophetic ministry, it can often be confirmation to what God is already saying to you, or perhaps you need to hold on to it and wait, allowing God to elaborate on it, and open the right doors at the right time. Always remember, though, that every prophetic word needs to be "weighed", you should never act on a prophecy alone. "This *will be* the third *time* I am coming to you. "By the mouth of two or three witnesses every word shall be established" (2 Cor. 13:1).

- **Your discernment** - Learn to recognise the witness of the Holy Spirit in your life and His "quickening" in your spirit. "However when He, the Spirit of truth, has come, He will guide you into all truth; for He will not speak on His own *authority,* but whatever He hears He will speak; and He will tell you things to come" (John 16:13).

- **Your leaders** - Leadership will often recognise God's call on your life when you cannot. Therefore consult with them before stepping out; when you feel God is leading you in a specific area, or if you are uncertain about where God is leading you. "Obey those who rule over you, and be submissive, for they watch out for your souls, as those who must give account. Let them do so with joy and not with grief, for that would be unprofitable for you" (Heb. 13:17).

- **Your faith** - Be willing to step out in faith in what God says; don't limit Him. If it is His call on your life He will also equip you. He is not looking for your ability, but your availability. "Now may the God of peace who brought up our Lord Jesus from the dead, that great Shepherd of the sheep, through the blood of the everlasting covenant, [21] make you complete in every good work to do His will, working in you what is well pleasing in His sight, through Jesus Christ, to whom *be* glory forever and ever. Amen" (Heb. 13:20-21).

HOW TO PREPARE FOR YOUR MINISTRY:

Preparation in our gifting involves being a part of the Body; submitted and teachable. It is vital that as we prepare ourselves, we build relationships, and grow in knowledge and spiritual understanding of our role and the roles of others. Therefore you must be willing to:

- **Be submitted** - Your ministry needs to be submitted to your leadership - they are God's delegated authority over you, but also God's gift to you. Usually they will encourage you, but sometimes will have to bring correction to you. A call to ministry is like a seed, it has all the ministry potential within it, and as you allow God to nurture it, it will grow and develop. You will rarely receive a full blown ministry immediately; God will teach you things along the way, trust Him. Ministry carries responsibility; therefore all ministries will need periods of mentoring to be effective. "Giving thanks always for all things to God the Father in the name of our Lord Jesus Christ,[21] submitting to one another in the fear of God" (Eph. 5:20-21).

- **Be obedient** - The only way to respond to the call of God is by loving, servant-hearted obedience. God wants you to respond to His call and to fulfil the ministry He has given to you. Jesus gave the greatest example, "Let this mind be in you which was also in Christ Jesus, [6] who, being in the form of God, did not consider it robbery to be equal with God, [7] but made Himself of no reputation, taking the form of a bondservant, *and* coming in the likeness of men. [8] And being found in appearance as a man, He humbled Himself and became obedient to *the point of* death, even the death of the cross" (Phil. 2:5-8).

- **Be dedicated** - You have to be totally dedicated to your calling. Never lose sight of the call of God and His purpose for your life. "I beseech you therefore, brethren, by the mercies of God, that you present your bodies a living sacrifice, holy, acceptable to God, *which is* your reasonable service. [2] And do not be conformed to this world, but be transformed by the renewing of your mind, that you may prove what *is* that good and acceptable and perfect will of God" (Rom. 12:1-2).

- **Be teachable** - In order to develop your ministry to its full potential, you have to be teachable and willing to take correction. It is essential to be trained in the ministry. This happens most effectively alongside others who are skilled and experienced in the ministry God has given you. "Listen to counsel and receive instruction, that you may be wise in your latter days.[21] There are many plans in a man's heart, nevertheless the Lord's counsel - that will stand" (Prov. 19:20-21).

- **Be disciplined** - In other words, stay within your calling. Learn to be who you are in your gifting. Don't try to be someone else or emulate their ministry. "Do you not know that those who run in a race all run, but one receives the prize? Run in such a way that you may obtain *it.* [25] And everyone who competes *for the prize* is temperate in all things. Now they *do it* to obtain a perishable crown, but we *for* an imperishable *crown.* [26] Therefore I run thus: not with uncertainty. Thus I fight: not as *one who* beats the air. [27] But I discipline my body and bring *it* into subjection, lest, when I have preached to others, I myself should become disqualified" (1 Cor. 9:24-27).

- **Be reconciled** - Your ministry will never be in isolation, but working in unity with other members of the Body of Christ. God builds teams. It is important that your relationships with fellow Christians are right and that you can learn to work together. "Endeavoring to keep the unity of the Spirit in the bond of peace" (Eph. 4:3).

We are living in incredible times, and God has placed each one of us in a unique position. Whether you are young or old, whatever your race or gender, whatever your upbringing or background, whatever your ability, whatever your present circumstances, you have been appointed and anointed to be a Kingdom representative, "solutionist and enforcer.

God does not always choose the most likely, or the most talented to bring blessing to the Body of Christ and the world. "But God has chosen the foolish things of the world to put to shame the wise, and God has chosen the weak things of the world to put to shame the things which are mighty" (1 Cor. 1:27).

For the Early - First Reformation Church, ministry development happened through discipleship. There was ongoing equipping taking place, with new believers being mentored by and learning from those who were more mature in the faith. The emphasis today in this Third Reformation; is on getting back to that biblical foundation. It's time for you to rise up and take your place!

You can find a detailed teaching on all the New Testament Gifts and Ministries as well as an online assessment to discover your gifts and callings on our website: www.reformation3.com

CHAPTER 7: REFORMING CULTURE – RECLAIMING THE 7 MOUNTAINS OF INFLUENCE

The heart of God has always been the transformation of society. The fact is, however, that in order to transform cities, regions and nations, we need to reclaim the 7 Mountains that shape each area's culture. The cry of the Third Reformation Church is that God's people must become strategic or else they will become irrelevant. When Jesus called us the salt of the earth, He meant that we are the ones that slow the process of moral and societal decay. For salt to slow the process of decay, it has to be in direct contact with the meat. The message of the 7 Mountains is meant to put us back in our place as salt and light to the world.

In other words, a church that is strategic and relevant will not just focus on what happens within the four walls of the church building...the mid-week Bible Study and Sunday services, but will also focus on our daily involvement and interaction in society as well. We have to become a people that know how to shape society by being involved and going for positions of high influence in the spheres that shape that society. Every person will find themselves in one or more places on the 7 Mountains. God is using this message to awaken us to become strategically positioned as Kingdom influencers in all of these areas. It is a "now" revelation to the Body of Christ and it will challenge many long-held paradigms held by the Church.

Have you ever struggled with or thought that there must be something more to the Christian life - some greater purpose than just "trying to keep holy" and wait for the rapture?   Clearly your salvation experience gave you a one-way ticket to heaven; but if you were like me...I still had a whole lot of living to do!

The Church has been so busy preaching on proclaiming a message of the Gospel that brings forgiveness of sins and security about your eternal future, that they have neglected the message of the Gospel of the Kingdom. The result of this is that we have abdicated our God-given responsibility to God's world, which He still loves (John 3:16); to teach and bring it under the influence of His Kingdom.

The problem, when the Church only preaches about sin, Sundays and the "sweet by and by, when we shall meet on that beautiful shore";

people have no vision, no God-given purpose for what to do with the rest of their lives (Prov. 29:18). This is where the Gospel of the Kingdom comes in. Jesus' first, last and main message was the Kingdom which is much larger than what the Church has typically addressed. This is the issue of the day. This Third Reformation will facilitate a major transitional shift in the mind-set of the Church to regain the lost emphasis of the fullness of the Gospel of the Kingdom as Jesus taught it to include the discipling of whole nations:

(Matt. 28:18-20) "And Jesus came and spoke to them, saying, "All authority has been given to Me in heaven and on earth. [19] Go therefore and make disciples of all the nations, baptizing them in the name of the Father and of the Son and of the Holy Spirit, [20] teaching them to observe all things that I have commanded you; and lo, I am with you always, *even* to the end of the age." Here we see clearly that our responsibility in obedience to the Great Commission is to **preach the Gospel of Salvation** and **teach the Gospel of the Kingdom** to bring about the cultural transformation of nations.

All of us can attest to the fact that in recent years we have seen the most rapid moral decline happening in our world. The culture we inherited from our forefathers is literally disintegrating before our eyes. The challenge we must answer, is what kind of world are we leaving for our children and grandchildren? Martin Luther said, "A Gospel that does not deal with the issues of the day is not the Gospel at all." It is a mistake to believe that the culture will shift because of a church revival. **Revival and Reformation must run together continually** over the generations and the Church has to be equally committed to both. Our Mandate is to fulfil **two Scriptural Commissions**: (Gen. 1:26-28) - the original covenant that shows us why God created us and our mission on the earth, and (Matt. 28:19) - we are to disciple nations.

Over the years the Church has gradually withdrawn from its place of influence on these mountains leaving a void now filled with darkness. When we lose our influence we lose the culture and when we lose the culture we fail to advance the Kingdom of God. Our generation now stands in desperate need. It's time to fight for them and take back the mountains of influence.

- The **Mountain of Business** is the foundation on which all other mountains are established and where resources are consecrated for the Kingdom of God or captured for the powers of darkness. This Mountain represents the source of provision in this world to meet man's physical needs and his need to subdue while he lives on the earth. God, as the Source and the Provider of all things; has entrusted these skills and abilities to us (Deut. 8:16-18). The Mountain of Business also provides the wealth or supply for the other mountains to exist (Gen. 1:27-28; 2:15). The Mountain of Business is the result of man fulfilling this God- given decree.

- The **Mountain of Government** is where evil is either restrained or endorsed. It provides rules, regulations and power over our lives. According to Paul, government is "ordained by God" (Rom. 13:2) to promote justice, restrain evil, and protect the people under its care (Rom. 13:3-4). As the children of the Kingdom of God, we must start to infiltrate the systems of government in positions where it counts, such as law making. We must get Kingdom influence back into local, regional and national government. We must be a prophetic voice to help bring God's Kingdom agenda back into law and policy making processes that will affect the future destiny of our nations.

- The **Mountain of Family** is where either the blessing or a curse is passed down to successive generations and where Satan wants to divide and destroy. At the foundation of every culture is the family. Tragically, we are living in times when family break-ups have now reached epidemic proportions. The Mountain of Family is the most important area of influence that needs to be refocused, reconciled and restored because it affects every other area of influence in communities and society as a whole.

- The **Mountain of Religion** is where people worship God in spirit and truth, or they settle for religion and ritual, or find other things and ideas to worship. God never gave man a religion, but an opportunity for a personal relationship with his Creator. For decades this is the only mountain that the Church has been concerned with. We have been content to stay there because we were led to believe that it is the only place God wants us to operate in but there are six other mountains/spheres of influence. God's vision for His Church is so much bigger!

- The **Mountain of Media** is where information is interpreted through the lens of good or evil. Media gives verbal and visual expression to the Mountains. It is one of the most effective ways that we can influence today's culture. We must reclaim the mountain of media to spread the Gospel of the Kingdom. Media is not just a form of information but a way to bring transformation to mind-sets, values and priorities that shape a nation!

- The **Mountain of Education** is where truth or lies about God and His creation are taught. Humanism and atheism have been the enemy's primary weapons to invade this sphere and has taken dominion over this mountain. The consequence of which has been a shaping of the minds of our children and young people with a life philosophy that is opposed to the Word of God. Our assignment in the 21st century is to reclaim this mountain (Prov. 22:6).

- The **Mountain of Arts and Entertainment** is where we express and celebrate the things in our life that either brings glory to God or man. This realm is also where true Godly values and virtues are either affirmed or distorted. This mountain includes arts, music, sports, fashion, drama and every other way we celebrate or enjoy life. I believe that innovation and originality is one of the hallmarks of God's Kingdom people because our God is a creative God (Gen. 1:1; Heb. 11:3) and because we, having been created in His image, are creative beings. In this Third Reformation God desires to showcase the inexhaustible supremacy of His creativity on the Mountain of Arts and Entertainment as we allow Him, once more, as in previous generations, to move freely through the creativity and passion of His people. This is essential to effectively communicating the Gospel to our culture.

Why has the Church allowed so much territory to be stolen and so much societal influence to be usurped? We have to correct our theology and face the fact that we got it wrong! Jesus always referred to the Gospel of the Kingdom, not the Gospel of Salvation! In essence, without realising it, the Church has left out 90% of the Gospel and kept only 10% - therefore only the introduction to the message has become the whole message. The consequence of this misapplication of truth has resulted in a Gospel that was split between what was considered spiritual and what was considered material. To repent means: Changed thinking! We must regain a correct understanding of the Gospel of the Kingdom! Reformation will come when we rediscover a faith that influences our thinking and actions in every area of living!

The tragedy that arises out of this unbiblical split thinking is that so many gifted people are sitting in the pews of our churches today wishing they had received a "real" calling to be a pastor or a missionary. They feel they would be more "spiritual" if they had received one of these callings. They may even secretly feel that they are not called to be pastors or church workers because they are less worthy. Unfortunately sometimes leaders use this as a means of manipulation and control. This is one of the consequences of unbiblical teaching; that the "secular" is bad and the "sacred" is good.

This is not theologically correct. We have to restore the biblical understanding, that if you are called by God to give your working life to family, or government, or business, or science, or teaching, or arts, or communication, you are not called to a lesser vocation than pastoral ministry. Your calling is equally from God, equally vital to that of those called to serve the church full-time. To fulfil the call of discipling the nations will require every believer, in every sphere of society, to become God's Kingdom representatives, by reaching their world!

(Isa. 2:2) "Now it shall come to pass in the latter days *that* the mountain of the Lord's house shall be established on the top of the mountains, and shall be exalted above the hills; and all nations shall flow to it." According to biblical expositors; a mountain as a prophetic symbol indicates either a kingdom or a government which amounts to the same thing due to the fact that a kingdom is a form of government. Therefore I believe it is correct to interpret the meaning of (Isa. 2:2), that the government of the House of the LORD shall finally, when He returns, have pre-eminence over all levels of human governments.

The Gospel of Salvation focuses on reconciliation alone. This should not in any way be minimized, but the Church has taken this mountain by itself, made disciples and occupied this territory. We have defended it and thought that our primary role was to protect it from invasion. In actual fact, nobody is trying to invade this mountain...mostly people are not concerned or interested in it, because they no longer see its relevance. The Church has barricaded itself in and spends all its time and energy guarding its perimeters. This often pointless "parading" results in a lack of purpose, causes restlessness and causes the occupiers to begin battling among themselves. The Gospel of the Kingdom when correctly applied removes these erroneous battle lines and enables us to see the greater vision. We are called to bring salvation and transformation of the systems of this world; namely the other mountains (Rom. 12:2).

(2 Tim. 3:1-9) "But know this, that in the last days perilous times will come: [2] For men will be lovers of themselves, lovers of money, boasters, proud, blasphemers, disobedient to parents, unthankful, unholy, [3] unloving, unforgiving, slanderers, without self-control, brutal, despisers of good, [4] traitors, headstrong, haughty, lovers of pleasure rather than lovers of God, [5] having a form of godliness but denying its power. And from such people turn away! [6] For of this sort are those who creep into households and make captives of gullible women loaded down with sins, led away by various lusts, [7] always learning and never able to come to the knowledge of the truth. [8] Now as Jannes and Jambres resisted Moses, so do these also resist the truth: men of corrupt minds, disapproved concerning the faith; [9] but they will progress no further, for their folly will be manifest to all, as theirs also was."

This passage articulates for us what happens when the Church abandons 6 of the 7 mountains of societal influence. Africa, for instance, is actually one of the most evangelized and most Christian continents on earth but it also has the worst poverty, the worst epidemics, the worst civil wars and the worst combined economy of any continent on earth. The alarming thing is that these crippling social issues massively increased after they had been evangelized. When we consider the reason for this, it becomes clear that only the mountain of religion was conquered, the rest were left without godly influence...without righteous leadership.

We have focussed only on making converts rather than mobilizing converts to go into the high places, the places of influence. When God's people take what God has given us and go into a situation, we become solutionists, we create solutions to problems. This is how we build a platform to speak into culture and disciple a nation. Leaders of countries with epidemics are not looking particularly for a Christian solution, but if a Christian becomes part of the solution then their Christian principles and values have a platform of credibility that can touch an entire nation. The same principle can be applied to every other mountain.

The Kingdom of God is not some esoteric, mystical realm but it is a tangible quality of life – a state of righteousness, peace and joy in the Holy Ghost (Rom. 14:17). It is relevant to and impacts every sphere of life. Believers are called to go into ALL the world - ALL the systems, as a positive and influential element. The question to ask ourselves is; do we have supernatural access and answers to problems? The answer is yes! Can we press into heaven to get economic and social solutions? The answer is yes! Can we become a force that can literally transform culture? The answer is yes! So what's stopping us?

Just as every believer has a ministry and giftings, I believe each are called to at least one of these mountains. We have to be committed as churches to mobilize an army of ambassadors into these 7 Mountains...to equip men and women to "take their mountain". We must serve as gatekeepers of the high places or mountaintop of these arenas with Kingdom values and priorities. (Rom. 5:20) "But where sin increased *and* abounded, grace (God's unmerited favour) has surpassed it *and* increased the more *and* super abounded" AMP.

What is your mountain of Kingdom influence? Perhaps you have more than just one. What are you doing to equip and enable yourself to climb it? My challenge to you is, waste no more time...step into your calling! Be a reformer! Shape your culture into His Kingdom culture 'on earth as it is in heaven!" Influence those around you! Transform the marred and distorted value systems! Heal the broken land! Think big...Disciple nations! You will be amazed at where God will take you, the people He will connect you to, and the doors of opportunity He will open up for you, when you make yourself available!

CHAPTER 8: REFORMATIONAL EMPOWERING - YOU HAVE AN UNCTION...YOU HAVE AN ANOINTING...IT'S THE SAME ANOINTING JESUS HAD!

Jesus said in (Luke 4:18-19) "The Spirit of the Lord is upon Me, because he has anointed Me to preach the gospel to the poor; He has sent Me to heal the broken-hearted, to proclaim liberty to the captives and recovery of sight to the blind, to set at liberty those who are oppressed; [19] to proclaim the acceptable year of the Lord."

In this scripture we see something very significant: we see that Jesus knew exactly what He was supposed to do and we see that Jesus knew that He was empowered to do what He needed to do. In other words, Jesus was consciously aware of a supernatural endowment...that's the anointing. Part of this reformation is the understanding that the purpose of God is that every one of His saints would be so consciously aware of this anointing, that every single one of us could say "the Spirit of the Lord is upon me!" This is not simply an expression or figure of speech, but we're talking about the tangible, manifested reality, of the power of God resting upon your life!

In Old Testament times, the anointing would only come upon certain people at certain times, for a specific task or purpose. That was a shadow; a type of the anointing that was going to come upon Jesus and through Him to us, by the power of the Holy Ghost! Today, the Holy Spirit dwells within us (John 14:16), "And I will pray the Father, and He will give you another Helper, that He may abide with you forever". "Do you not know that your body is the temple of the Holy Spirit *who is* in you, whom you have from God, and you are not your own?" (1 Cor. 6:19). (1 John 2:27) tells us that the anointing now abides/remains in us, "But the anointing which you have received from Him abides in you, and you do not need that anyone teach you; but as the same anointing teaches you concerning all things, and is true, and is not a lie, and just as it has taught you, you will abide in Him".

We have to get a fresh revelation that this anointing was not just for Jesus, nor is it just for; apostles, prophets, pastors, teachers and evangelists; it's for every born-again child of God. It is the will and purpose of God that every blood washed, Holy Ghost filled believer could say with the same certainty and the same authority as Jesus did, "the Spirit of the Lord is upon me because he has anointed me".

(Acts 10:38) tells us how God anointed Jesus of Nazareth with the Holy Ghost and with power, who went about doing good and healing all that were oppressed of the devil for God was with Him! He was the pattern and so now we say, "we are anointed with the Holy Ghost and with power, we go about doing good, healing all who are oppressed of the devil, for God is with us".

Jesus in His physical body is no longer here, but the anointing is still here. We are now His hands and His feet. We are His voice on the earth. We are anointed to carry on His work! We are anointed to preach the Gospel, to cast out devils, to heal the sick, to deliver the bound and the oppressed and set the captives free! (1 John 2:20) says, "But you have an unction...from the Holy One", (verse 27) says "but the anointing which you have received from Him..." You have an unction, you have an anointing, and it is the same anointing Jesus had!

(Acts 3:1-8) "Now Peter and John went up together to the temple at the hour of prayer, the ninth *hour*. ² And a certain man lame from his mother's womb was carried, whom they laid daily at the gate of the temple which is called Beautiful, to ask alms from those who entered the temple; ³ who, seeing Peter and John about to go into the temple, asked for alms. ⁴ And fixing his eyes on him, with John, Peter said, "Look at us." ⁵ So he gave them his attention, expecting to receive something from them. ⁶ Then Peter said, "Silver and gold I do not have, but what I do have I give you: In the name of Jesus Christ of Nazareth, rise up and walk." ⁷ And he took him by the right hand and lifted *him* up, and immediately his feet and ankle bones received strength. ⁸ So he, leaping up, stood and walked and entered the temple with them - walking, leaping, and praising God."

Peter and John looked at this poor crippled beggar sitting at the temple gate asking alms from any who would pass by and they were moved with compassion for him. Compassion and pity are two different things. Pity may look, feel sorry for, perhaps even cry, but compassion acts, compassion changes the situation. And when they said, "look at us"; it was because they knew they had not only the compassion, but the capacity to change this man's situation! We have to grasp this. We've prayed it, we've prophesied about it, we've sung about it, but we've not grasped it.

That's what part of this reformation is all about...it's not just the Church, you and me having the revelation that we are walking around with the same Spirit, the same power that raised Jesus from the dead, living on the inside of us 24/7. It's more than just a revelation; many of us have had the revelation for years. It's about moving from revelation to activation!

We've got to move beyond just the prayer and the prophesying, as important and necessary as they are and we've got to begin to be a demonstration on the earth of Him, of His Kingdom, of His rule and reign. To be, not just priests who will stand in the gap and weep and travail, like Jeremiah, for our generation, but to be the priests and kings of the Kingdom; in other words to rule and reign with Him.
Not only to legislate in the heavens and make decrees, but to follow that up with action. To go in that anointing and do the works of Jesus, now! We've got to be Jesus in the courtroom, Jesus in the classroom, Jesus in the boardroom. To be Jesus in the coffee-shop with that person you've known for ten years, but never shared the Gospel with. To be Jesus in your neighbourhood, to take that mountain of influence that He's given you. To say like Caleb, "Give me this mountain!" (Josh. 14:12).

Peter and John knew that this supernatural life-force was in them and they also knew that they had the ability to transfer; to release that power to others. "Silver and gold have I none, but such as I have". There's the key, "such as I have!" Peter and John were consciously aware that they had in their possession, a power greater than themselves. "Such as I have, I release, I transfer, I give to you". Peter took him by the right hand and lifted him up and immediately his feet and ankle bones received strength. Was it God's will to heal this man and make him whole? We know it was. Why didn't it happen sooner? Because no one had passed his way, with the knowledge, the revelation, of possessing the power to change his situation!

I'm telling you today that it is still the will and purpose of God to heal the sick, deliver the bound and the oppressed and to set the captives free. But I'm also telling you, that nothing is going to happen, until we realize that we are the carriers and the conduits of the power of God and we start laying our hands on the sick and we start lifting them up in Jesus' Name and we start casting out devils. There are people, just like this crippled beggar, all around us, every day and even though God wants them well and whole, they will die; lost, sick and afflicted, if we don't recognize that we are the channels of God's power and if we don't take His power to them!

The Spirit of the Lord is upon me because He has anointed me, not to make me feel good or give me goose bumps, but the anointing is on me...to prophesy, to lay my hands on the sick, to rebuke disease and to cast out anything the devil has brought upon you!

(1 Pet. 2:24) says, "Who Himself bore our sins in His own body on

the tree, that we, having died to sins, might live for righteousness - by whose stripes you were healed". When Jesus died on the cross, He paid for everything (Heb. 9:28). You haven't got to earn it; you haven't got to deserve it. Be healed! Be restored! Be made whole! Walk in Jesus' Name! See in Jesus' Name! Hear in Jesus' Name!

There are some, who are perhaps not physically crippled but they are emotionally crippled. Life has hurt them, life has disappointed them. Like Mephibosheth (2 Sam. 4:4), they have been "dropped", let down, wounded by people who were supposed to nurture them and love them and so now, even in their adult life, they have become emotionally handicapped. They can't receive and respond to love. They have addictions and unhealthy dependencies, because nothing fulfils that void that was left in them. They have irrational behaviours and responses, because they became stunted at some point of trauma in their life and so they stopped growing and maturing emotionally, in that area.

With some people, they may not be physically deaf or blind, but they went through some "stuff" spiritually that they didn't understand. They thought they got a word from God and they did, but they didn't discern the time and the season (1 Chron. 12:32), because for everything there is a time and a season (Eccles. 3:1). So they birthed an" Ishmael" and they're living daily with the consequences and so now they refuse to see or hear the truth, that will set them free.

The anointing is there, right where you are, to heal you, now! The anointing is there to deliver you and set you free! It's time to become a carrier, a conduit, a channel for this anointing, to let it flow through you, out there, to where it's needed, to be a Reformation Three Revolutionary!

CHAPTER 9: REFORMATIONAL LEADERSHIP – RECLAIMING THE LOST AND HIDDEN LEADERS

In (Titus 1:5), Paul reminds Titus of the reason he left him in Crete, to "set in order the things that are lacking" and he also charges him with appointing elders or leaders in every city. There is a revolution in this verse! Paul is putting in place a strategy to impact and transform an entire nation, by affecting every city, town and village!

(Titus 1:1-5) "Paul, a bondservant of God and an apostle of Jesus Christ, according to the faith of God's elect and the acknowledgment of the truth which accords with godliness, [2] in hope of eternal life which God, who cannot lie, promised before time began, [3] but has in due time manifested His word through preaching, which was committed to me according to the commandment of God our Savior; [4] To Titus, a true son in *our* common faith: Grace, mercy, *and* peace from God the Father and the Lord Jesus Christ our Savior. [5] For this reason I left you in Crete, that you should set in order the things that are lacking, and appoint elders in every city as I commanded you."

I want to deal in this chapter with the subject of "Reformational Leadership". I want to begin by making a revolutionary statement, but after over twenty-five years of full-time leadership; in churches, in business, on university and school boards, in community projects, it is something I am totally convinced about. It is also something that is absolutely biblical and yet we have allowed the world's system and the world's thinking, to erode away, this truth and it's so fundamental to who each of us is as a man or woman of God, is the fact that every one of us is a leader!

This has been one of the greatest deceptions of the enemy that has crept into the Church and robbed so many of God's people, of their callings and destinies. If we are truly going to see this third, crucial reformation of the Church, this is a paradigm shift that is going to have to happen, first, or we'll just talk about it and theologise about it but the revolution won't take place! Why are we using...this kind of terminology? A revolution, according to Webster's Dictionary, is "A violent attempt by many people to end the rule of one government and start a new one". Jesus said, in (Matt. 11:12) "And from the days of John the Baptist until now the kingdom of heaven suffers violence, and the violent take it by force."

We're obviously not talking about physical violence but we are talking about a spiritual battle; spiritual force! We're talking about a system of government or rule, that is ungodly, that is unbiblical and that is ruling in the heavenlies, above governments of nations and world rulers that we have got to topple and take down, before we'll see change on the earth!

The apostle Paul said in (Eph. 6:12) "For we do not wrestle against flesh and blood, but against principalities, against powers, against the rulers of the darkness of this age, against spiritual *hosts* of wickedness in the heavenly *places.*" We're not just dealing with that, we've got to deal with an unbiblical form of government within the church, which has caused it to become; ineffective, passive, weak, undiscerning, lethargic and lukewarm!

We've got to dismantle it and remodel it, according to the Book of Acts and the New Testament Church! That's what this Third Reformation is all about! And it's going to take a new breed of leadership; I'm calling it "Reformational Leadership". Most people, even within the Church are convinced that leadership refers only to a specially chosen, professionally trained few! Our cultures and oftentimes our environments, that have shaped us and moulded us, have all but extinguished the belief that we can lead! That's why our world is in the state it's in! Leadership has been delegated to governmental and civic leaders, many of whom are not God-honouring.

Fathers have abdicated their leadership responsibility in the home. Teachers have abdicated their leadership responsibility in the classroom. That's why there's anarchy; no respect, no discipline, no order but chaos and that's the devil's playground! That's why his agenda is to tear down and destroy the leadership potential and anointing of people, especially God's people.

I believe that part of this Third Reformation, is to restore to the Church, its leaders. The church should never be short of leaders because we're all called to lead; to mentor, to disciple others. Each person has the potential, more correctly, the obligation, to develop the leader within them. The Church, the world, needs them, with their specific gifts and unique leadership anointing. They owe it to their generation. If we are going to change the world...every person has to start believing they are a leader!

We have to return to the biblical pattern that leadership is above all, service! How do you become a leader? By serving! How do you serve? You serve with your gift! So, servant-leadership is simply being willing to serve with your gift at every opportunity. Jesus addressed this in (Mark 9:33-35), "Then He came to Capernaum. And when He was in the house He asked them, "What was it you disputed among yourselves on the road?" **34** But they kept silent, for on the road they had disputed among themselves who *would be the* greatest. **35** And He sat down, called the twelve, and said to them, "If anyone desires to be first, he shall be last of all and servant of all."

Don't wait until the senior leaders give you a fancy title or promotion! Clean the bathrooms and serve...make tea and serve...stack the chairs and serve...join the stewards team and serve...sing in the choir and serve...cut the grass and serve! That's where it has to start! We will never release or promote anyone in a leadership role in our churches or ministry, who does not, first, have a servant-heart or a servant-attitude! Jesus was our prime example, (Mark 10:45) "For even the Son of Man did not come to be served, but to serve, and to give His life a ransom for many".

We have to re-establish the principle in the Church, that leading is an ability possessed by every person! We have to empower people to realize: You were created to lead...you have leadership potential...you were designed to fulfil your assignment because God put you on this earth to meet a specific need no one else can meet! There are things only you can unlock and open up. There are people only you can reach; only you can touch!

I tell our new converts, before they get "infected" by all of the misperceptions of leadership and ministry that exist in the church: The first question you ask yourself after getting saved is: "Who am I? What is my gift? How and whom can I serve?" And then you roll up your sleeves and say, "Here I am, Lord, use me!"

Now if we're going to be able to start a revolution and bring about this shift and re-establish God's government, God's order and God's agenda in the Church and through it, bring a demonstration of God's Kingdom; to our neighbourhoods, our communities, our nations and the world, I believe there are at least 12 qualities that every Reformational Leader must have:

- **Be Full of the Holy Spirit** - We see a practical example of true spirituality and biblical leadership throughout the book of Acts. As we read, we are repeatedly referred to people of great maturity and Christ-like character. The Book of Acts, though, is not so much a record of the acts of men, but rather the Acts of the Holy Spirit through the lives of everyday people, like you and me, who dared to believe God and live out His Word. Ordinary people who accomplished extraordinary things because they were endowed and empowered by the Holy Spirit.

In the book of Acts the Holy Spirit is referred to some 46 times. Nearly every chapter mentions His ministry. It records for us how God calls all kinds of people to all kinds of ministries and, whether it is a call to witness or to serve tables or to solve a problem or the need of guidance, the work of the Holy Spirit is present and crucial. It is imperative that those serving and leading in the church be men and women who first are filled with the Spirit.

(Acts 6:1-4) "Now in those days, when *the number of* the disciples was multiplying, there arose a complaint against the Hebrews by the Hellenists, because their widows were neglected in the daily distribution. [2] Then the twelve summoned the multitude of the disciples and said, "It is not desirable that we should leave the word of God and serve tables. [3] Therefore, brethren, seek out from among you seven men of *good* reputation, full of the Holy Spirit and wisdom, whom we may appoint over this business; [4] but we will give ourselves continually to prayer and to the ministry of the word."

- **A Positive Attitude** - The fact is, once you discover your purpose you have a positive attitude. There is no place, in a revolutionary church for pessimism and negativism. As a Reformational Leader you don't indulge in it and you don't allow others to. Once you allow it in it's very hard to get rid of it. It's like a virus; it spreads, it infects and it contaminates. It weakens the vision and the unity, that's why...we give no place to it! "Finally, brethren, whatever things are true, whatever things *are* noble, whatever things *are* just, whatever things *are* pure, whatever things *are* lovely, whatever things *are* of good report, if *there is* any virtue and if *there is* anything praiseworthy -meditate on these things" (Phil. 4:8).

  A Reformational leader puts positive energy into everything. They want everyone to succeed. This unwavering commitment they have keeps people going, through good times and bad. It has been proven that if people do not believe that they can succeed their efforts will wane. Therefore, they not only set the example, but constantly motivate their followers by listening, encouraging and enthusing.

- **Passion** - I have found that when you know who you are and you're operating in your gifts, you will find that there is a divine momentum that comes... you will have the passion; you will have the energy to get the job done! Whinging, whining leaders, "Oh I've had such a bad week, I hardly had time to prepare...too tired...too busy" you need to question whether you're operating in your calling or not, because you can never inspire others from that place! (Phil. 2:13) says, "For it is God who works in you both to will and to do for *His* good pleasure".

You see, all great achievements start with passion. The greatest motivator that inspires creativity and mobilizes to action in the life of any person is the thing that they are most passionate about. Your passion is your unique frame through which you view the world. It not only fashions who you are, but also the kind of people you connect with and what opportunities you seek. You know that you are passionate about something when you wake up every morning knowing that this is what you've been called and destined to do. Passion is what shapes your purpose in life!

Commitment is necessary and ultimately will complete the task, but passion goes beyond commitment. Passion is the thing that compels and constrains us to go above and beyond just what is essential or required. This can be evidenced in every area of life...our marriage, our career, our personal development and of course our spiritual walk. Church leaders who are passionate about God and ministry are constantly pursuing more effective ways to reach each new generation with the Gospel.

There are talented people everywhere, but passionate people stand out from the crowd. The fact is, though, that passion doesn't just happen because we are drawn to something or have a vested interest in it; passion is cultivated by choice and determination. Our world, really is lost...people are lost (Isa. 53:6) and now, more than ever, the world needs people with more than just gifting or talent, but real passion; because passionate people inspire others to change - they become God's reformers! In (2 Tim. 1:6) Paul encourages Timothy, "For this reason I remind you to fan into flame the gift of God, which is in you". It's time to get re-fired, re-commissioned and passionate about the destiny God has for us and for His Church today!

- **Vision** - One of the most important qualities any leader must have is vision. Vision not only gives direction but also builds essential cohesion amongst those being led. Without vision, it is not possible to strategically communicate with people or win their confidence and commitment to follow. People will trust you as a leader if you can articulate to them precisely where they are going, how they are going to get there, how it will look when they get there and what they need to do to get there.

Reformational Leaders see the big picture. They see the short-term and long-term goals. They are people of faith. They believe - with God it's possible, "We can do it...we can make it...we can achieve it!" Like Joshua and Caleb they instil that confidence in others (Num. 13:30). They keep people focussed on the vision...they keep people connected to the vision. "Where there is no vision, the people perish: but he that keepeth the law, happy is he" KJV (Prov. 29:18).

- **People Skills** - Leadership is influence, therefore leadership can be nothing but people orientated. Leadership that does not put people first is not sustainable. If you are cold and only task oriented it doesn't matter how effective a strategist you are, if people don't think you care or that you're concerned about them, they won't connect with you.

  As a Reformational Leader, you realize that everybody is important, and as Jesus loved the Church (Eph. 5:25), so you have to love His Church! (Eph. 4:15-16) "But, speaking the truth in love, may grow up in all things into Him who is the head - Christ - [16] from whom the whole body, joined and knit together by what every joint supplies, according to the effective working by which every part does its share, causes growth of the body for the edifying of itself in love".

- **Integrity** - If you are a person of integrity then what you say in public is the same as what you do in private. It is upholding a code of moral values that you not only communicate but also display in everyday life. You have to be true to God and true to yourself...never, ever step over that line. It will always have consequences! People will get hurt...the church will get hurt...you will get hurt. One of the devil's names in scripture, is the "father of lies" (John 8:44). He is the "deceiver", "Beelzebub" (Matt. 12:27)! That is one of his greatest tools of destruction in the Church and as leaders we must never give place to it! We have to always walk in integrity. (3 John 1:4) says we must always be "walking in the truth"!

Leadership is all about trust. The majority of people have been hurt, let down and disappointed, by people in authority. Therefore, in many instances, trust isn't just given, it has to be earned! So be consistent...do what you say you're going to do. It sounds so simple but one thoughtless oversight that you assumed was insignificant can be crushing to somebody who's learning to trust again, after being hurt by a leader! (Matt. 5:37) "But let your 'Yes' be 'Yes,' and your 'No,' 'No'. For whatever is more than these is from the evil one".

- **Responsibility** - True Reformational Leaders do not stop until the job is finished! I remember once at a leadership workshop I was giving to a large group of leaders from several of our churches, saying to them, "I'm giving you all fore-notice that if one more leader tells me God told them to stop, resign or withdraw from an area of ministry or a job they haven't finished, I'm going to lay hands on them! I won't do it suddenly because that's not biblical! I'll tell you to duck, before I slap you!" This was during a time of great transition in our ministry; from a local and city mandate, to a national and international one. I told them, "My Bible tells me that the work that God starts, He finishes! (Phil. 1:6) My Bible tells me that what He said He'll do, He'll do" (Num. 23:19).

True leaders don't stop until the job is finished. They never make excuses. They may give reasons but never excuses. (2 Cor. 8:10-11) exhorts us "And in this I give advice: It is to your advantage not only to be doing what you began and were desiring to do a year ago; ¹¹ but now you also must complete the doing *of it;* that as *there was* a readiness to desire *it,* so *there* also *may be* a completion out of what *you* have".

- **Self-Discipline** - The word Jesus used for His followers was "disciples" (Luke 9:1) and discipleship by its very definition requires discipline! Effective leaders are self-disciplined. They are on time, they're well-prepared, and they're well-presented. It's not a matter of any old thing will do, but they strive for excellence and they always give of their best. The Bible says in, (Heb. 11:4), that by faith Abel offered a "more excellent" sacrifice to God than did his brother, Cain. We read in that account found in Genesis, chapter 4, that Abel brought the first and the best of his flock to offer to God. Abel offered God his best. He gave an "excellent" sacrifice. Obviously, we do not sacrifice animals as an offering to God, anymore. The Bible makes it clear that the sacrificial system was finished with Jesus Christ being the perfect Lamb that was slain for the sins of the whole world.

However, we are now asked to sacrifice something much greater: our lives. (Rom. 12:1) says, "I beseech you therefore, brethren, by the mercies of God, that you present your bodies a living sacrifice, holy, acceptable to God, *which is* your reasonable service." As born-again believers we are to offer our lives as a "living sacrifice" to God. Abel offered up an "excellent sacrifice". Are we offering up an "excellent" life as a sacrifice to God?

In all areas of life, in "whatsoever ye do", we are to strive to live as an excellent "living sacrifice". We do not strive in order to bring honour to ourselves, but we strive for excellence so that, "they may, by *your* good works which they observe, glorify God in the day of visitation" (I Pet. 2:12). One definition for self-discipline is "Denying yourself certain things to achieve something else!" The Bible calls it "taking up your cross" and "counting the cost"...that's what true leaders do!

(Luke 14:27-33) "And whoever does not bear his cross and come after Me cannot be My disciple. [28] For which of you, intending to build a tower, does not sit down first and count the cost, whether he has *enough* to finish *it* - [29] lest, after he has laid the foundation, and is not able to finish, all who see *it* begin to mock him, [30] saying, 'This man began to build and was not able to finish'? [31] Or what king, going to make war against another king, does not sit down first and consider whether he is able with ten thousand to meet him who comes against him with twenty thousand? [32] Or else, while the other is still a great way off, he sends a delegation and asks conditions of peace. [33] So likewise, whoever of you does not forsake all that he has cannot be My disciple."

- **Submission** - In the military everyone has a higher authority and it's the same in the army of God. Leaders must be followers, too!

Particularly in this Third Reformation where the Lord is re-establishing the Five-fold Ministry, we have to be prepared to submit to those who are in spiritual authority over us, even as they submit to the Lord. "Obey those who rule over you, and be submissive, for they watch out for your souls, as those who must give account. Let them do so with joy and not with grief, for that would be unprofitable for you" (Heb. 13:17).

The moment, as a leader, you have a rebellious heart, a rebellious spirit or attitude, immediately you disqualify yourself! Even if you disagree, it has to be with honour. God so hates rebellion, He says it is as witchcraft (1 Sam. 15:23), because its root was in the heart of Satan when he rebelled against God. Rebellion opens the door to every demon of deception and division! When rebellion enters the heart of someone the wall is up, and it's almost impossible to get them to hear truth!

Remember, submission and humility operates together. The humble leader assumes that they do not have all the answers and they listen to people's opinions and explanations. Humble leaders look for the opportunities to learn and make others feel valued.

A true leader does not care who gets the credit! Reformational Leaders are more concerned about results, than rewards and recognition. They are not insecure; they are not threatened by other people's giftings. Insecure leaders lead by casting shadows over other ministries, rather than mentoring and encouraging. Effective leaders know who they are and what they're supposed to do!

- **Resilience** - There will always be set-backs but a good leader has to be able to bounce back. (Prov. 24:16) says the righteous person may fall or stumble seven times but they get back up again! I tell leaders, "Whatever you are facing or going through, right now, is qualifying you for leadership. This is no time for a 'pit stop' or 'time out'. Learn as you go through, because God is preparing you. He's not finished with you, yet. It's on-the-job training for greatness!" (James 1:3 & Rom. 5:3) says the trying of your faith produces; patience, perseverance and endurance. Reformational Leaders are not afraid of change. Reformational Leaders have the courage to do what is right when no one else does and to make 'the call', when no one else will make a decision. (1 Cor. 16:13) "Watch, stand fast in the faith, be brave, be strong!"

Paul encouraged Timothy, in (2 Tim. 2:8-10) to endure the hardships for the sake of the believers, "Remember that Jesus Christ, of the seed of David, was raised from the dead according to my gospel,[9] for which I suffer trouble as an evildoer, *even* to the point of chains; but the word of God is not chained. [10] Therefore I endure all things for the sake of the elect, that they also may obtain the salvation which is in Christ Jesus with eternal glory".

- **Growth** - True leaders are always growing, learning and developing. They have a hunger for knowledge. They want to study (2 Tim. 2:15). They're always reading and expanding their minds...they love the Word of God! There's no place for stagnant leaders in this reformational move of God! We need cutting-edge leaders who will inspire others to aim higher! Leaders with no relevant, current and up-to-date information are not leading the church up but down. (Prov. 12:1) says "Whoever loves instruction loves knowledge, but he who hates correction *is* stupid." A Reformational Leader is a creative leader. They love new approaches, suggestions and ideas; even when they are not their own! (Prov. 19:20) says, "Hear counsil, receive instruction, *and* accept correction, that you may be wise in the time to come." AMP

I have found that when a leader stops growing, the following happens - they:

- Lose their passion - they don't feel energized and inspired
- Become complacent, stop caring and lose interest
- Lose sight of their dreams and goals
- Stop believing in their ability to grow
- Feel irrelevant and lose their ability to motivate and influence others
- Become resistant to change
- Develop their own agenda, and finally;

- Become disengaged

- **Purity** - A leader who has hidden sin in their lives will never succeed in the long run. (Prov. 28:13) says, "He who covers his sins will not prosper, but whoever confesses and forsakes *them* will have mercy". Concealing sinful behaviours that we are unrepentant for may not affect us economically. In fact, we may even rake in more. Hiding your sin may not impact your professional life. In fact, more opportunities to ascend the corporate ladder may come. Continuing with undealt with sin may not impact your social life...no one may ever suspect or know.

The real consequences and damage, though, is to your heart. Sin will cause you to shrivel spiritually. Your desire to spend time with God will diminish. "Nevertheless I have *this* against you, that you have left your first love. [5] Remember therefore from where you have fallen; repent and do the first works, or else I will come to you quickly and remove your lampstand from its place—unless you repent" (Rev. 2:4-5). Your heart will become hardened, "For the hearts of this people have grown dull. *Their* ears are hard of hearing, and their eyes they have closed, lest they should see with *their* eyes and hear with *their* ears, lest they should understand with *their* hearts and turn, so that I should heal them" (Acts 28:27).

Your spiritual discernment will be dulled, "'Seeing they may see and not perceive, and hearing they may hear and not understand;

lest they should turn, and *their* sins be forgiven them" (Mark 4:12). Your spiritual passion will become cold which will inevitably lead to Luke warmness, "So then, because you are lukewarm, and neither cold nor hot, I will vomit you out of My mouth" (Rev. 3:16), and you can be sure that sooner or later, your sin will find you out (Num. 32:23). Sin always produces consequences, "For the wages of sin *is* death, but the gift of God *is* eternal life in Christ Jesus our Lord" (Rom. 6:23).

You have to keep your house in order and set a standard of holiness in your life, or your leadership will never produce results; fruit that lasts. "You will know them by their fruits. Do men gather grapes from thorn bushes or figs from thistles? [17] Even so, every good tree bears good fruit, but a bad tree bears bad fruit. [18] A good tree cannot bear bad fruit, nor *can* a bad tree bear good fruit. [19] Every tree that does not bear good fruit is cut down and thrown into the fire. [20] Therefore by their fruits you will know them" (Matt. 7:16-20). There is also a clear biblical code of conduct for "elders" - spiritual leaders and "deacons" - practical ministry leaders in (1 Tim. 3:1-13).

CHAPTER 10:   CONCLUSION

HOW "MINISTRY" HAS CHANGED FROM ONE GENERATION TO THE NEXT:

This reformational move of God has come at the neediest, most critical time in the history of the Church. But the Lord says, "For My Name's sake I am going to do a mighty deliverance." I believe that, as a result, this generation is going to see great numbers coming to the Lord and it will not happen through hype, advertising or prominent names.

We have to stop focussing on the past and instead look toward the future. I, like you, am so thankful for what the Lord has done for and through His people throughout Church history; but He desires to do a new thing...He said so Himself (Isa. 43:19)! I believe as we step into this next great reforming move of God, what we are going to see emerge is one of the most devoted and dynamic generations of men and women and young people, full of the Holy Ghost and fire and ready to make Church history!

You may sometimes wish you had been at Pentecost...one of those in the Upper Room, but I believe, if Scripture is to be true, that the best days of the Church are still ahead! What God wants to do for us is more powerful than anything seen in the past. At this moment,

He's saying to His Church "I want to increase your power; I want to increase your resources, and increase your influence and authority." (Acts 9:31) "Then the churches throughout all Judea, Galilee, and Samaria had peace and were edified. And walking in the fear of the Lord and in the comfort of the Holy Spirit, they were multiplied." (Acts 16:5) "So the churches were strengthened in the faith, and increased in number daily."

We can't schedule a revival or an awakening. You can't hold conferences or write books to make it happen. It happens when God's people intercede and cry out to Him in prayer! It happens when God's people break out of their complacency and comfort zones and step out in faith and obedience and do what He told us to do. It happens when they "repent", "change their thinking and direction" and return to Jesus' commission to preach the Gospel of Salvation AND teach the Gospel of the Kingdom...and then demonstrating that in all of their life!

MINISTRY TO THE "MILLENNIALS":

There is an increasing sense of restlessness in the Church. The generation that's coming of age in the Church today is not wired like their parents were...they don't want to sit on the side-lines of ministry. They are hardwired to want to be a part of something that is larger than themselves. They want to see a different world...and they want to be a part of the change process. They are the "Millennials", by definition, those born between 1980 and 2000. This generation of young adults is full of optimism and hope. In fact, 96 percent of them agree with the statement, "I believe I can do something great!" But the majority say individual prominence is secondary to helping the community and accomplishing things for the greater good.

A growing number of people, like them, in our pews are awakening to the fact and asking the question as to why Christianity, as lived out in the Book of Acts is so radically different from what the Church portrays as the norm today! "When do I begin to see the Holy Spirit manifest Himself through the gift He gave me?" Millennials value churches where each person is empowered to participate. Millennials refuse to sit on the stands as spectators. They want to be participators. They want to be part of the action and yet statistics reveal that they are leaving the church in droves because most churches haven't figured this out, yet.

As Reformational Leaders we have got to figure out how to empower them and give them a chance to play a meaningful role in the Kingdom of God...God's work in the world. They are ready to follow the right kind of leadership; leaders who are operating in a transformational capacity - and ones who aren't afraid to get their hands dirty. They are looking for leaders who won't just give instructions but work alongside them. They are looking for team leaders. They are our greatest asset in reforming the Church to address and meet the needs of today's world...and ensuring that Jesus finds faith on the earth, when He comes (Luke 18:8)!

I believe that this should be the Church's greatest hour!

THE MANDATE OF REFORMATION3 NETWORK OF MINISTRIES & CHURCHES

We believe God has called us to help shape and model a significant shift in the Church; how the Church sees the Church, how the world sees the Church and how the Church functions and operates. This shift will see it break free from many of the man-made religious, unbiblical models and structures, that particularly in the context of Europe and the western world have caused it to lose ground, lose relevance, lose credibility and momentum!

We've seen groups, that have rightly discerned what is lacking in the church, spring up and they've become almost sectarian. Why? - Because they've become disconnected from the local church. Why? Because the church hasn't made room for them! But that is the role of the church; that's what the church should be doing!

Part of the function, I believe, of our REFORMATION3 NETWORK OF MINISTRIES & CHURCHES is to provide a meaningful place of connection, relationship and coherence for ministries, pastors and churches so that together, in Kingdom partnerships, we can reach our generation, shape our nation and change our world!

Please visit our website for more information on how you can connect with us and the teaching and training events and materials that are available: **www.reformation3.com**

ABOUT DR BRAD NORMAN:

Dr Brad Norman is a biblical academic, pastor, teacher, visionary, mentor and motivational speaker. He preaches a real and relevant word with a strong apostolic emphasis. He holds a Seminary Diploma in Divinity, a Bachelors in Theology, Masters in Biblical Studies and a Doctor of Ministry degree. In addition to pastoral ministry, he has served on the faculty of two theological colleges, lecturing in Systematic Theology and Pastoral Ethics.

His message of 'Enlightened Empowerment' and 'Present-Day Truth' has brought invitations for him to minister in many nations, in conferences and leadership training events. Throughout his 25 years in Ministry, Brad has sustained a spirit of excellence and integrity. He is passionate not only to see believers equipped and local churches mobilized in their mandate and mission, but also for leaders and pastors serving on the front-line.

He was born in Durban, South Africa and raised up under his spiritual parents, Dr Fred and Ps Nellie Roberts. After relocating to the United Kingdom in 2000, he has been instrumental in the successful establishing of several churches under the covering of SALVATION FOR THE NATIONS INTERNATIONAL CHURCHES which he, together with his wife, Wyona, established in the January of 2003.

Since then they have been sought out by many churches, church leaders and pastors who are seeking relationship and apostolic partnership. This has led to the establishing of REFORMATION3 NETWORK OF MINISTRIES & CHURCHES; which offers ministry accreditation, as well as training and mentoring programmes seeking to restore a true biblical model for a fully functional Five-fold Ministry in the church today. The online REFORMATION3 COLLEGE OF MINISTRY & LEADERSHIP offers a 1st Year - Certificate in Biblical Studies and a 2nd Year - Diploma in Ministry programme. Visit the college at: **www.reformation3college.com**

Brad and Wyona live in Hertfordshire, Greater London, where they have their ministry headquarters and conference centre; Salvation House. They have a son, Devon and a daughter, Bianca. In addition they have two adopted children; Tia and Bella who are possibly the most spoilt Bichon puppies in the world! For more details and information on their itinerary or how to invite them to speak at your conference or church event please visit the ministry website.